Cover photo: Brimston(

Taken in 2010 at the outer corner of a fie

at the very edge of Bath and W

where I was attending New Wine, a large Christian conference,

the photo was one of the highlights of my week.

Probably the best butterfly picture I've ever snapped,

it's often reminded me of how the beauty and dignity of hidden treasures

are to be found on the edges rather than in the limelight of society

or of any community.

Coming Home for Good: Personal Reflections on Homelessness

Dedicated to the memory of Frank Nuttall, father of this prodigal son who

came home

Author's Note and Acknowledgments:

Some names and a few other minor details have been changed to protect privacy. Otherwise, the narrative accounts of my life experiences are entirely true, honest and accurate, *as remembered, interpreted and told from my own subjective, individual viewpoint.* Other people involved would inevitably recall or view the same events differently. If we were to hear their perspectives as well, they would create complementarity rather than conflict, not negating but shedding new light on my own accounts.

The postmodern idea that what is true for you may not be true for me is often viewed with at least suspicion, if not disdain, by other people of faith who see truth as an objective set of rigid facts that they believe in. While I agree to a degree, the truth is that truth is so much broader than this. Subjective experience is real and true to the subject experiencing it.

The beauty of narrative accounts and phenomenological research which have gained increasing popularity in recent years is that they give validity and importance to the real lived experience of real people, affirming them as valued individuals in a world of faceless numbers.

My thanks go to everyone mentioned, whether by name or not, in the narrative sections of this book, all of whom have played a part in the rich tapestry of my life, ultimately all for good.

And finally, thank you to Van Morrison, whose music has been a near-constant companion and inspiration throughout the writing of this book.

CONTENTS

Preface

Nobody chooses homelessness, do they?

Well, most don't. *Most* homeless people don't choose to live on the streets – they land up there because life has handed them a raw deal from the start. Becoming homeless is usually the cumulative effect of adversity and affliction. Life and bad fortune have conspired against them, often from childhood onwards, in some cases eroding their ability to make what we think of as wise choices and eventually leaving them without roof or base.

But there *are* some who choose homelessness as a means of escape: for example, from domestic or sexual abuse, or violence.

Others opt out of "the system" because they don't feel able to cope with the trappings of bills and belongings, relationships and responsibilities. Some are trying to escape from themselves.

I was one of those. The underlying reasons behind such a choice are sometimes not *so* different from those who are forced into homelessness. Choosing to live on the streets or on the road is an "unusual" life choice. I hesitate to say "abnormal", as one person's normal is another person's weird, and vice versa.

I'm convinced, in our target-driven world that would mould us into uniformity, of the critical need to accept and nurture every individual's unique identity, with all our idiosyncrasies and (often creative) eccentricities. A paradigm shift is needed in our education, arts, friendships, communities, care services and employers.

These words of Jean Vanier, founder of the L'Arche communities, ring instinctively true with me:

"Only occasionally have some societies recognized

that those who are 'abnormal' are in some ways prophetic,

pointing to a world of truth

which transcends their experience of normality."[1]

Someone who chooses a transient lifestyle, like many artists and geniuses, may be a "normal kind of eccentric" and point us to a different kind of reality, a different kind of "normal" from the one we're used to. However, living on the road or on the streets by choice may equally be an outward symptom of *spiritual* and *psychological* homelessness, as it was for me. Probably not many travellers or homeless people would put it in those terms, but I'd suggest we all need a home not of bricks or mortar, but rather the eternal arms of Love, a spiritual and psychological place of belonging. A place of security for the heart and soul, which will inevitably work its way outwards in a positive spiral of recovery, relationships, and the resources to face the challenges of life. Oh, and physical re-settlement too.

But it's not just those without a physical home who experience spiritual homelessness.

Ours is a beautiful but broken world, with often fragile relationships, fragile minds and souls. Many feel disconnected in a myriad of ways. They may have a physical home but no experience of feeling secure in themselves, no sense of what their place is in this world, no sense of meaning or purpose, or of belonging in a disjointed society. To them, the world may seem an intimidating, daunting, even threatening place.

---

[1] Jean Vanier, *The Broken Body* (London: Darton, Longman & Todd, 1988), 48.

For me, a spiritual homecoming brought about a sudden and unexpected homecoming to purpose, to my human father as well as to a heavenly Father, to a caring career, to a wife and family, to a physical home and, of almost greatest importance, to myself.

It probably goes without saying that what worked for me isn't going to work for someone else in the same way. Nevertheless, it is my hope that my story will connect in some way with you, whatever your life experience.

This book is therefore not simply an account of my own journey home, but is interwoven with reflections on life, faith and homelessness, drawn from anecdotes and episodes along the way, including my personal and professional relationships over the years with homeless people, from life on the street to working in a homeless health service.

I hope you will find these accounts and reflections inspiring, thought-provoking, or at the very least informative, and bear some relevance, whether or not you've ever had any encounters with literal, physical homelessness.

Because it's my belief that there's a homecoming for *everyone*.

PART ONE:

A HOMELESS SOUL

1: No home for my soul

> *The ache for home lives in all of us,*
>
> *the safe place where we can go as we are.*
>
> Maya Angelou

I didn't run away from home till I was 16. I guess I'd been waiting for an opportunity, an excuse to trigger my escape.

From the age of about 11, till nearly 22, all I ever dreamed of doing in life was to bum around the world, to live life free, on the road. Forever.

No responsibilities

    No possessions

        No home

            No hassles.

                An itinerant life.

I was turned off by society's toxic treadmill that I'd witnessed first-hand in my own family's disenchanted lives – a microcosm of humdrum western civilisation.

In 1980, when I was 14, I eagerly listened to The Specials as they reflected my scorning of education and the work ethic in *Rat Race*[2].

At sixth form, in '82 / '83, when we were supposed to be thinking about choosing careers or universities, all I could think about doing was roaming the world, a free spirit. With dreams of busking across the continents, I tried to learn guitar, but gave up after the first couple of blisters. I lacked both dexterity and perseverance.

---

[2] The Specials, *Rat Race*, 2 Tone Records, 1980.

I'd lie on my bed listening to the melancholy lyrics and haunting guitar outro of Queen's *Spread Your Wings*[3] – the first record I ever bought (with the fast & fabulously furious *Sheer Heart Attack* on the B-side) – on my old Boots record player, dreaming of spreading my own wings.

Life on the road was perhaps an unusual ambition for a young, middle-class boy – born, it seems, out of a sense of rootlessness, home not being home. You could call it psychological homelessness. I do. Not feeling like I belonged in the place that should have been home. But also, not even *wanting* a home. Somewhere in my psyche, home was anathema.

More significantly, I'd describe it as *spiritual* homelessness: that feeling, familiar to many, of not belonging in the only kind of society we know; and of life being devoid of meaning.

The world of music, and the arts in general, are permeated with plaintive cries of spiritual or existential anguish, often as expressions not just of the artists' own personal experience but of the *world* as they see it.[4]

As an atheist since early childhood, having no faith, no reason for living or basis for existence, I was left floundering in this universe. Like a swift on the wing, no home for my soul to hang its hat.

Some time in my mid-teens, I watched a programme about the Big Bang: how an infinitesimally small piece of matter somehow combined with an infinitesimally small dot of energy, to form a monstrously ginormous explosion that kick-started the Universe.

The programme left an indelible impression on me. It all seemed implausibly plausible, but where did that impossibly small fragment of

---

[3] Queen, *Spread Your Wings*, EMI, 1978.
[4] Such as: Bruce Springsteen's *Hungry Heart*; *Hole in My Life* by The Police; and Coldplay's *Talk*, to name but a few examples.

matter and that impossibly small iota of energy *come from*? The programme didn't answer that question. I don't think it even asked. The question bugged me for years. It hounded me. I just couldn't get my head round it, and went through a stage of believing the Universe was just a figment of its own imagination.

Through my childhood and teens, I grappled with the questions of existence – of the Universe, of myself, in fact the existence of existence, leaving me in a state of spiritual freefall.

The ache for home, of which Maya Angelou spoke, undoubtedly burned in my heart, but I had no awareness of it. The ache found its expression in a restless, wild urge to escape.

***

So the opportunity came one day, for this 16-year-old atheist with a homeless soul to leave his dead life behind and chase the dream of life on the road...

School was over for the day and as usual I was hanging around in Uckfield on my way home to Buxted from school in Lewes, when I was caught shoplifting for the *n*th time. Same old, same old. It was only a bar of coconut ice, for goodness sake. I probably could have paid for it, even, but my whole lifestyle was one of cheating, lying, and stealing. I cheated in exams, lied my way out of things, and saved money by theft. It was partly habit, partly ethos. Get what you can out of life for free.

The shop owner, knowing who I was, was going to ring my parents. Not being able to face them *yet again* on the issue of shoplifting, and feeling like I had nothing to lose, it seemed the perfect opportunity to live the dream and take to the streets.

So after dumping my school bag in a public toilet, I walked up the A22 out of Uckfield and started hitching for London, slightly scared, mostly buzzed. But dusk was soon falling and no one stopped for me.

As the evening darkness enveloped the Wealden countryside on the edge of Ashdown Forest, I knew I'd have to wait till the morning to try hitching a ride again. Creeping into a greenhouse in a nearby garden, I tried to settle down on the dank concrete base amidst the plant pots and trowels, but as the cold, dewy night descended over the thin jacket I was wearing, sleep proved impossible.

So about 5am I ventured back out, thumb extended over the dark, empty, rural road. Incredibly, somebody soon stopped. A friendly commuter. I told him I was going to London to see Madness in concert and had left home extra-early in case hitching proved difficult. He seemed to believe me. I wasn't a huge Madness fan – it was just the first band name that popped into my head – although I *was* going One Step Beyond!

I'm not sure what part of London he dropped me off at, but I was completely lost. I went looking for the places I vaguely knew – Trafalgar Square, the West End – to go and live on the streets there, but had no idea how to get there or how far I was from those places. It was still early morning; I nicked a bottle of milk off a doorstep and bought a cold meat pie in a corner shop: just enough to keep me going, as I wandered through the city streets.

Eventually, a grimy street sign uninvitingly informed me I was somewhere around...*Putney*? To this day, I have no idea where *Putney* is.

Then the lightbulb moment dawned. When the realisation hit me that I was a very long way from central London and entirely lost, I thought, "I'll go to Brighton, where I know my way around, and live on the streets there. *And...*I can pop in at home on the way, to pick up a bag and some warmer clothes."

So, off I hitched again, and managed to make it back to Buxted by the afternoon. Thankfully for me, the house was empty and I crept in. But while I was throwing some belongings into a bag to take with me to Brighton, the police turned up.

My parents had, of course, reported me missing the previous night and spent some time talking with the police, who had now returned, hoping to catch my parents at home to ask some more questions. To their surprise, they found me instead!

It was a classic case of good cop / bad cop. As we sat round the kitchen table, the "bad cop" forcefully lectured me on the immorality of stealing, attempting to badger me into agreeing that shoplifting was just plain *"wrong!"*, while the "good cop" tried to empathise, to understand what had gone wrong at home and why I'd felt the need to escape.

By this stage of my childhood I'd become somewhat alienated from those who were supposed to be close to me, so the caring police officer's attitude made a big impression.

My parents came home, more concerned than cross on this occasion.

So, my first escape only lasted 24 hours and I never made it to Brighton. For now I was to stay at "home", but with still no home for my soul, until the next opportunity to escape presented itself some 3 years later.

2: Homesick blues

Reality is just a crutch for people who can't handle drugs.
Robin Williams

As I cycled down the country lanes of Buxted, delivering newspapers to the large detached houses with detached people and manicured gardens, I'd recall the words by Public Image Ltd's *No Birds (Do Sing)*[5] – a cynical take on the sterile fakery of suburbia – that seemed to reflect my more rural but no less conservative surroundings.

No inner city deprivation for me.

After the swift rise and demise of punk, in which the Sex Pistols had exploded into my young-teen consciousness like an unexpected friend on a lonely day, I remained a loyal devotee of John Lydon and his new band Public Image Limited in the ensuing years. PiL's songs, that continued to express punk's disenchantment with the establishment in the late '70s / early '80s, became comforting echoes in my head.

The mostly wealthy mid-Sussex village of Buxted bore a cold veneer of Daily-Mail-reader affluence that *probably* masked all manner of untold middle-class secrets.

But my childhood in this cold, aloof village wasn't *all that* bad – compared with many, perhaps most, of the homeless people I've met – even if it was saddening, maddening, bad enough to make me want to escape.

Up to a third of homeless people grew up in care[6], many removed from traumatised beginnings and/or addicted parents, then passed from pillar

---

[5] Public Image Limited, *No Birds (Do Sing)*, from the album *Metal Box*, Virgin Records, 1979.

to post, never knowing the unconditional love, affection and stability of family life needed to nurture robust individuals.

Most homeless people grew up in some sort of corrosive combination of economic, emotional, relational and/or spiritual poverty[7].

These childhood experiences of trauma and deprivation have a tendency to set off a destructive and unique spiral of complex needs such as mental health disorders, learning difficulties, drug use and/or alcoholism, resulting for some in a revolving door of repeat homelessness that's all but impossible to break out of.

My childhood, on the other hand, was a far cry from material poverty. In 1967, when I was two, and life in the Nuttall household was still relatively happy as far as I know, we moved from Uckfield, the small Sussex town where my Dad worked as a lawyer for the Magistrates Courts, to the nearby sleepy village of Buxted.

My parents, whose marriage was the culmination of a whirlwind holiday romance, had a detached 4-bedroom house custom-built, surrounded on three sides by a huge garden where my sister Ruth and I enjoyed happy adventures as young children.

We had several skiing holidays in the days when only the well-off went skiing (in fact, it's probably still only the well-off who go skiing). Ruth and I were sent to private schools.

It should all have been lovely. But the subsequent 10-plus years of acrimony and verbal abuse that filled the house, as my parents stayed

---

[6] Crisis, *Research briefing: Young, hidden and homeless* (London: Crisis, 2012).
[7] Poverty is usefully defined in these four ways by Martin Charlesworth and Natalie Williams in *The Myth of the Undeserving Poor: A Christian Response to Poverty in Britain Today* (Guildford: Grosvenor House Publishing Limited, 2014).

together "for the sake of the kids", must have shattered their dreams of idyllic village life.

It's an old joke: "I'm feeling homesick – sick of being at home." But for many children, the sentiment can be dead serious. As it was for me. And from an early age, I wanted out.

The relatively privileged lifestyle was all I knew. But even from a young age, being brought up with the subtle delusion that we were somehow better than others – more an unfortunate and unintentional hangover of my mother's colonial upbringing in the former Dutch East Indies (now Indonesia) than Dad's influence – I was aware of our family's self-evident detachment from ordinary people. It went against the grain of this child's instinctive urge to be part of a larger tribe.

Dad was from a working/middle-class family in Saafend (as he liked to pronounce Southend) and, despite having risen to his respected, professional position, liked to drink with the rough and readies in a threadbare old pub, ironically called the New Inn, in nearby Hadlow Down. An incongruence strongly frowned upon by Mum!

You can take the man out of Saafend but you can't take Saafend out of the man.

On the one hand, my upbringing bred a general sense of disconnection from society; on the other, it perhaps contributed to my individualism which, although often seen as a Western pitfall, can equally be a positive, innovative trait.

In terms of early dysfunctionality, my story is not unusual, but it *is* individual, with some scenic twists and turns of both physical and spiritual adventure.

When I compare my past with the lives of the homeless people I work with, I'm aware that I haven't undergone half of the trauma many of them have been through, but also that I experienced enough of a sense of rejection and disconnection to have a healthy degree of empathy with them.

I've sometimes wondered why I never developed any serious addiction, as many of the people I work with have. It may simply be down to genetic predisposition. After all, my Dad, in his 50s, decided to quit smoking one day, and never picked up a cigarette again.

Or perhaps the *relative* stability of being with both parents and relative material privilege protected me against addiction to the big habit-forming chemicals of alcohol, tobacco and Class A drugs that crossed my path. Over the years, however, I did develop a number of other, more psychological than physical, dependencies.

To this day, coffee, chocolate and work are some of my biggest addictions. Before you scoff at the innocuousness of these attachments, let me explain: I mention them because there are people (I'm sure you're not one of them) who see themselves as immune to addiction and look down on those with obvious dependencies, viewing those sufferers as "weak" or even label them as "low-life", as I've seen on social media. We sometimes fail to see that we're all in the same boat; that, as psychiatrist Gerald May put it, "to be alive is to be addicted"[8], whether to chemicals such as ethanol, caffeine or sugar, or to behaviour patterns and emotions like lust, anxiety, guilt and shame.

---

[8] Gerald May, *Addiction and Grace* (London: Bravo Ltd, 2007).

Recently, I had to re-evaluate my life and work patterns with the help of a counsellor, when a prolonged period of stress exacerbated by my workaholic tendency and over-devotion to my job came to a head. Workaholism has similar roots to other addictions and can be just as destructive as alcoholism.

I'm not cured of my propensity for dependency.

Addiction is one symptom of the crisis of disconnectedness that's all around us. The more disconnected we are from family, friends and society, the more likely it is that we will form unhealthy bonds with heroin, cocaine, alcohol, gambling, money, pornography, mobile phones or some other addictive pattern.

In my teens, my own disconnectedness, my homesick blues, gradually drew me towards various kinds of addiction, including shoplifting, cannabis and an infatuated kind of romance.

Robert Palmer couldn't have got it more wrong in *Addicted to Love*[9]: not only because real love, as I've now come to understand it, is the one thing we cannot be addicted to, but because it's the one *cure* for our addictions.

Such a shame that the musical genius that was Robert Palmer will forever be remembered not for his earlier and far more interesting hits like *Looking for Clues* and *Johnny and Mary*[10], but for that awful song with its misleading message and infamously sexist video!

Infatuation and lust, which the song is actually about, are addictions that chain us; while love is always giving, always *free* to give.

According to Gerald May,

---

[9] Robert Palmer, *Addicted to Love*, Island Records, 1986.
[10] Robert Palmer, *Looking for Clues* and *Johnny and Mary*, Island Records, 1980.

> "Although addiction is natural, it severely impedes human freedom...and makes us slaves to our compulsions. Grace, the freely flowing power of divine love in human life, is the only hope for true freedom from this enslavement."[11]

Love will not enslave, nor will it ever tear us apart. Love will only ever set us free.

***

My motto in my teens was "I'll try anything once, except heroin" – and I pretty much lived that out.

Although, like a sheep, I followed the teenage mandate to get drunk at weekends, and tequila was my soothing companion during my time on the road, alcohol never *really* bothered me. In fact, from the moment of my life-changing experience of the Holy Spirit in 1989 (described later), I've never been tempted to get drunk again. That's not a boast, simply an observation. I've never had that experience of one drink leading to another and another. Seeing the grip alcohol has had on so many people I know, and the resulting process of physical and spiritual dying, I count myself fortunate in that respect.

Like most kids, I smoked, and again chain smoking went with the territory when I embarked on the road at age 19 onwards. But in 1987, at the age of 21, a couple of months before my first step towards Christian faith, I decided to quit (cigarettes, that is, not cannabis yet).

It was a slightly unusual reason for quitting. Hitch-hiking to Portland, Oregon, to try and get some work with Ray Galloway, a painter / decorator I'd worked for previously, to save up some money to continue

---

[11] Gerald May, *Addiction and Grace* (London: Bravo Ltd, 2007).

my travels, I knew that if I carried on smoking, the friends I'd made previously in Portland would be constantly bumming fags off me and I'd end up spending all my cash on cigarettes. So I quit, and never went back to it. Just like that. Like my Dad had done, only a lot younger.

Once in Portland, I was snorting methamphetamine ("crystal meth", or "crank" as they called it) with these friends, as I had been on a previous stay with them. I watched these young people getting hooked, spending all their money, not eating.

A young couple I knew were expecting a baby, who I later learned was taken into care. Not only did I not want to end up like them, the crystal meth never really did it for me, and I felt lucky not to get hooked. For one thing, it wasn't my kind of buzz – I liked the soothing escapism of weed too much. Stimulants just weren't my thing then, although the most popular of stimulants – coffee – is my thing now.

Any kind of abuse or neglect experienced as children can cause a stunting of emotional (and even physical) growth, so those emotionally scarred by abuse, as a huge proportion of homeless people are, are likely to grow into adulthood lacking the psychological coping strategies needed to deal with life's difficulties and more readily turn to substances as a way of handling tough times than those who haven't experienced such traumas. Although I didn't experience the outright abuse that often triggers drug and alcohol addiction or mental disorders, the tense and bitter atmosphere at home sadly overshadowed any love and affection my parents may have attempted to give their children.

Relationally adrift, I bumbled clumsily from one girlfriend to another throughout my teenage years, with no clue how to be in a relationship, unknowingly looking for something they could never provide. As one girlfriend called out after me as I walked off in a huff down the road after a row: "It's not my fault you're insecure!" Well put.

In later life I came to recognise that Mum and Dad did their best to be parents, and that we were loved and cared for within their very human limitations.

At the same time it seemed obvious in hindsight that a difficult home life was the main antagonist in the ensuing pattern of disruptive, defiant behaviour and social ineptitude that developed through my childhood into my teens.

3: They paved paradise[12]

Everybody needs beauty as well as bread, places to play in and pray in, where nature may heal and give strength to body and soul.

John Muir, American environmentalist (1838-1914)

Kids deal with their childhood disaffectedness and traumas in different ways. Like most dysfunctional families, ours wasn't a culture where emotions were discussed. There was no openness, especially about the problems in the home. In our state of emotional illiteracy, feelings were suppressed.

My way of dealing with things was to walk and wander alone. Growing up in rural Sussex suited my introvert personality. There were a number of public footpaths that I'd be forever exploring, that trailed through wild woodlands and secluded fields, or along streams sparkled with fish and kingfishers.

I say "public" footpaths – there were also plenty of barbed-wire and electric fences scrambled over or scraped through, not to mention the odd shortcut through private gardens. Forgive us our trespasses...

From early on, I had the kind of boundless freedom unknown to most kids these days.

I happily trudged the muddy footpaths, and developed a love of nature – butterflies especially – that continues to this day. There were a lot more butterflies then, in the 70s. I'd collect, kill, set and display them in cases,

---

[12] A nod to Joni Mitchell, *Big Yellow Taxi*, Reprise, 1970.

until in my teens, my conscience suddenly kicked in, and collecting butterflies gave way to photographing them, as I still do now.

The Wealden countryside was my home from home. Or, rather, just *my home*.

Of special interest was a small, natural lake at the bottom of Redbrook Lane, that I often visited.

This narrow, bumpy, private road was named after the reddish-orange hue of the stream – fed by natural iron in the soil – that ran into the lake. While writing this book, I re-visited Redbrook Lane and walked down to the lake to see how much it had changed since I'd last seen it some 35 years earlier – whether it was still a wildlife haven or whether they'd built houses round it. Incredibly, it hadn't changed *at all*. The whole area was exactly as I remembered it – perhaps a little more overgrown, therefore still completely unspoilt and natural. It was such a joy to see it again, untampered by human development.

I'd sometimes go fishing there, on my own or with my school-friend Martin – never usually catching anything.

In the winter, when it was frozen over, my neighbour Tim and I would walk out on the lake, to generally mess around and try and break the thick solid ice with whatever objects we could find. Looking back, it was so risky and I'd hate the idea of my own kids doing anything like that – walking out on a frozen pond, with no one nearby to hear them if anything went wrong.

On one occasion I was there with Ruth, when we had the privilege of seeing a huge snake (at least, it's huge in my childhood memory) having some kind of duel with a stoat or weasel on the far side of the lake, before both animals eventually gave up and slipped away. It was one of the most

23

astonishing sights of nature I've ever seen. In fact, that incident, some 40 years ago, was, sadly, the last time I saw a snake in the wild.

Another time, I came across Elephant Hawk Moth caterpillars – weird and wonderful, elephant-grey leathery creatures with a trunk-like head – on willow herb, next to the lake. I took them home, reared them through to the striking purple and green adult moths, and released them into the wild. I've never come across these incredible caterpillars before or since. That's how special this idyllic site was to a budding young naturalist who found his home in the wilderness.

There was one other special place – a field less than half a mile from our house, that was swathed in butterflies each summer. I nature-watched there, collected butterflies and moths, and roamed about like the dreamer that I was. And in the woods nearby, I'd discover antique bottles that had been disinterred by the natural processes of time from a Victorian dumping ground.

Unfortunately, one day I set fire to the field...

It wasn't *entirely* deliberate. I was about 13 at the time, playing with fire – something my friend Martin and I used to do together. We'd make campfires, set light to cans of hairspray to make amazing flame-throwers, and throw things like gun cartridges on to the fire to see what would happen. Both our dads had shotguns – that's country life for you.

Martin and I were considered to be a bad influence on each other at school, and had to be separated in class. They were probably right. I'd say that it was more Martin influencing me than the other way round, as it was *he* who introduced *me* to smoking, glue-sniffing and pornography. On the other hand, I led the way when it came to shoplifting.

Both our parents seemed to think their son was the innocent party. When my parents discovered cigarettes in my coat pocket, I claimed they were Martin's. The same thing happened to Martin and he blamed me. Incredibly, both sets of parents seemed to believe their own child. So that was handy!

But this time I was on my own. I'd built a little fire, just for the fun of it, then tried to stamp it out, but it quickly grew out of control. The flames had taken hold of the brittle summer grass and wild plants, and there was no stopping it. I ran to the nearest house – its garden backed on to the field – and asked the owner, Mr Webb, who knew me and my parents, for a bucket of water. He looked out the back and quickly commented, "I think it's too late for buckets of water", dialling 999 as he spoke. The fire brigade were thankfully able to extinguish the flames with those big paddle-like beaters, but not until the flames had reached the edges of the field. One devastated meadow later...

I wasn't brave enough to admit to Mr Webb or the firemen that I'd started the fire deliberately – it just seemed such a stupid thing to have done – so I told them I'd been smoking (true) and had carelessly discarded a lit cigarette end (not true).

My Webb promised not to tell my parents about the incident as long as I promised not to smoke again until I turned 16. Of course, I went along with this brilliant deal, with no intention of keeping to it. Such was my young teenage immorality.

I cringe now at some of the petty crimes of my teens. As a 16-year-old I knocked on doors of a small neat, suburban close near our house with a bodged-together, home-made collection-tin, purportedly raising funds to save whales or dolphins or something. The money, of course, was for me.

Astonishingly, many residents seemed to believe me and obliged with their loose change.

I mention this to illustrate the unscrupulousness of my immaturity. I don't think I've ever told anyone about that tin-rattling escapade till now.

And the field – as far as I know, my parents never did find out about that, either. Phew!

I was sad for the field. My ethics did extend to caring for wildlife – the fiery incident taking place after the time I'd stopped collecting butterflies. And the wildflowers and grass grew back within a year or so – such is the resilience of nature. Well, maybe two years.

Sadder still for me, though, was the day I visited the field a few years later – I must have been away at boarding school and come back for the holidays – only to find the field was *gone*. Permanently. In its place was a small housing estate. It had become Britts Farm Road. The field was not just temporarily damaged this time, but decimated, destroyed. Gone forever.

They paved paradise and put up a housing estate.

I sat on the ground, incredulous, and cried.

I've felt that affinity with nature many times since.

When I look back at that moment in the late '70s, I see the start of the poet and dreamer in me. I mean, boys are meant to play football, get into fights or race motorbikes and cars, aren't they? Not me – I was fascinated by butterflies and cried over fields. Takes all sorts to make this world, eh? Nowadays, I don't need to escape from home (although sometimes when the kids are fighting, I might feel like it) but nature remains my hiding place.

Prayer and *meditation* in a place of natural solitude is just the perfect mix: a physical and spiritual place of rest and revitalisation away from the bustle of life.

And they can't pave prayer.

4: Great expectations

I tested in the top percentile for IQ, but I couldn't tie my shoes or really ride a bike without training wheels until I was almost 7.
Stephen Rodrick, journalist

IQs, somewhat out of favour these days, aren't everything they were once cracked up to be. However, in the early '70s, when I was tested at the age of 6 or 7 at Skippers Hill Manor prep school, my parents and teachers seemed to be somewhat gushing at my IQ score.

It was lower than the Mensa minimum and *undoubtedly* lower than the IQ of plenty of people I've met and worked with since. Nevertheless, my parents and teachers congratulated me that I was in the top 1% of the population in the intelligence stakes. It's natural enough for parents to bask in their kids' abilities, however much these attributes are down to luck and genetics rather than any effort on the part of their kids. As a parent myself, I'm sure I do it too.

But from early on, expectations were high: too high for me to live up to. We know full well now, if not then, that IQ only measures certain kinds of intelligence, sometimes referred to as "cognitive ability", and not necessarily emotional intelligence, creativity or practical intelligence, for example.

I was good at puzzles or problem-solving: cold, hard logic; the stuff of IQ tests. I discovered that I could excel at arithmetic, and the technical side of language – grammar, spelling, and written translation, but not *speaking* foreign languages.

I also found from pretty early on that I *really* struggled with handwriting, absorbing factual information and following stories, whether read by me or aloud by a teacher. Being aware now of dyspraxia in my family, I'm absolutely certain this played a part in my difficulties too.

The term dyspraxia is sometimes used interchangeably with Developmental Coordination Disorder, and many years ago was known as Clumsy Child Syndrome. In fact, my clumsiness was a cause of much chiding at home.

Like most things, understanding of and support for dyspraxia has come on leaps and bounds since my childhood, although even now teachers still sometimes seem to lack awareness of the condition.

Being placed in a class a year ahead of my age on the strength of my IQ and a couple of specific subjects served only to exacerbate my problems in other areas of learning, where I ended up struggling more than other kids in the class.

Many years later, in my teens, after moving from a public school with small all-boy classes where I was the best in my O-level year at French on account of technical language ability to Lewes Priory, a mixed comprehensive sixth form, it came as a shock to the system to find that many of the girls in my new school were far better at French than I was and seemed to be able to speak the language semi-fluently. Even at French, I wasn't as smart as I thought I was.

The only other boy in that French class was Madcat Alan (aka Luxy), who I'm still proud to call a great friend, even though he lives the other side of the world now. Back then, we'd skip French, to avoid the world's dullest teacher, in favour of cycling down to the Brighton arcades to play Pacman.

Despite my supposed brightness, I still seem to be completely unable to grasp news stories about wars and politics or anything but simple movie plots, or to retain any vaguely complex information – no doubt the reason why I've never developed a hunger for books and shy away from academia. As a nurse and prescriber, I struggle with the science side of my job and frequently feel inadequate with my hopelessly poor retention of medical knowledge.

I find it hard to understand how my wife can retain and process all sorts of useful information and useless trivia and remember what the weather was like last summer, making her a much better conversationalist than me, while she can't comprehend how I can easily memorise a 16-digit credit card number!

It sometimes feels as if there's some kind of neurological disconnect within this allegedly intelligent brain of mine.

As a young child, I was given a copy of *Great Expectations* – which I trawled through, reading and probably understanding every word, but took none of it in. It was like I'd set myself a challenge to complete the task for the sake of it. If I'd been asked afterwards what the story had been about, all I could have said was that there was a character called Pip. Apart from that, I didn't have a clue.

To be fair, I was too young for the Dickens classic. Even so, that memory now feels like an omen of the conflict I was to encounter with the great expectations that were placed on my future.

***

But back to early school years....coupled with the inconsistencies in my abilities were some relatively mild, but growing, behavioural problems. Over the years, I've tended to put these down to the problems at home.

I have a feeling, though, that it all started even before that. Teachers carried out all kinds of abuses back then, the likes of which wouldn't be allowed today – I hope. For example, at the age of about 5 or 6, there was an incident at St Nicholas' School in Uckfield, where I spent my first 2 years of education.

It involved me and another kid innocently playing in the classroom with a makeshift catapult we'd made out of small wooden building blocks, that sent other blocks into the air, and a ceiling light bulb somehow getting smashed in the process. It must have been a pretty damn fine machine we'd made, to fire missiles up that high!

Like a lot of boys, although I'm sure I played energetically, I clearly remember there was no deliberate naughtiness or destructiveness on my part. But as far as the teachers were concerned, I was very much at fault and was made to walk round the playground at break time with a cardboard sign pinned to the back of my jumper, that read "I am a naughty boy" – to the amusement of all the other kids. Talk about labelling. It was utterly humiliating and, as you can tell, it stuck in my memory.

The fact that I could read fluently before starting school didn't help, either. I remember learning to read at home with my Mum, and I don't think she was pushy. It just came together quite easily. One of my very first school memories involved the class slowly sounding out the letters "c-a-t-cat!" and other 3-letter words from books with one-word pages, as I sat there thoroughly bored, able to read whole pages of text with no problem. That boredom spelled disaster (pun intended) and no doubt played out as "naughtiness".

It seems highly likely that the "naughty" label stuck as a result of these early incidents instigated by boredom or sheer energy, particularly the cardboard sign episode. I guess I started to believe and live the label, as we tend to do.

In seeking out the best advice when it comes to raising our kids, my wife Janine and I have found Janet Lansbury's book on toddler discipline, *No Bad Kids*, immensely helpful. In the foreword, Lansbury writes:

> "As the title of this book states, in my world there are no bad kids, Just Impressionable, conflicted young people wrestling with emotions and impulses, trying to communicate their feelings and needs the only way they know how. When we characterize them as bad because we're frustrated, confused, or offended by their behavior, we are doing them a great disservice. It is a negative label, a source of shame they may eventually start to believe about themselves."[13]

In my case, the label was a physical, cardboard one.

Another episode stands out in my mind – one which in many ways was not at all unusual in its era but for me exemplifies the somewhat hidden problems I experienced with learning.

We had to write an essay on the Battle of Hastings. At 7 or 8, I was a year younger than most other kids in the class. I struggled at home to put something together. I think I was meant to have taken in some information that had been read to us in class. My parents had no useful encyclopaedias. And, sadly, it was to be about another 25 years till the internet arrived in family homes.

---

[13] Janet Lansbury, *No Bad Kids* (JLML Press, 2014).

My essay started: "Once there was a battle. It was called the Battle of Hastings…" After that, I was a bit stuck. I knew nothing else about the Battle of Hastings. How was I meant to know this stuff??!

My attempt at an essay consisted of those 2 short sentences, which I handed in. My two-sentence essay was read out to a guffawing class, the teacher joining in the laughter as she read it.

That was just one example of many in which my particular learning struggles, exacerbated by the effect of being in a class ahead of my age, triggered mockery from the other kids.

Of course, that kind of ridiculing in class was commonplace back then and, as for a lot of people, it knocked my confidence – in contributing in classroom situations and in learning generally.

***

The delicious irony of this anecdote is that some 30 years later, in 2004, I moved with my wife and kids from London to Hastings. I'd successfully applied for a post leading a primary healthcare service for homeless people, which I do to this day.

Hastings called me to join the battle against homelessness and complex needs. We still live in this scenic, culturally thriving town which has received repeated accolades throughout the national press over recent years and where continued regeneration and gentrification (for better or worse) have been doing battle with rising homelessness and deprivation, driven by Conservative policy that favours the already well-off and pushes the poor further into poverty.

I'm now fully engaged with the new Battle of Hastings.

And despite living here for over 13 years, I still can never remember who William or Harold was, or which side each of them was on. I just don't seem to be able to retain that kind of factual information, especially when given orally, like in that scenario at primary school.

***

I have no intention of exaggerating these challenges or to claim that I had or have a learning disability as such. Just to tell my own unique story, to recount the chain reaction of inherent difficulties with education and childhood events that led to my itinerant ambition and disconnection from society.

Although the greater proportion of homeless people experienced some form of childhood poverty, the homeless come from all walks of life, as you might expect. And when it comes to intelligence, there are of course no sweeping statements to be made. But many do have learning disabilities and challenges, including autism spectrum disorders (ASDs). In the 2015 East Sussex Homeless Health Needs Audit[14], which surveyed 285 individuals who were or recently had been homeless, including some of the people I work with, 21% responded that they had been told by a professional that they had a learning disability: *ten times* the proportion of the general population who are known to have a diagnosed learning disability.

Many of these individuals have mild difficulties, and may have received some support during their education. This, though, is likely to have stopped by the time they reached adulthood, leaving them to struggle independently with the challenges of managing tenancies, bills and the other demands of life. Homelessness is, sadly, an unsurprising outcome,

---

[14] East Sussex County Council and Homeless Link: *East Sussex Homeless Health Needs Audit* (East Sussex County Council and Homeless Link, 2016).

particularly where emotional or other kinds of abuse have been a factor behind the disability.

But, of course, homelessness can happen to anyone, whatever their intelligence. And, in this respect, Steven always springs to mind.

Steven had been a professional scientist, his intellect evident in his speech, and was (barely) living in a shelter on Eastbourne seafront in the early '90s. He was pleasant and articulate, and gratefully accepted flasks of tea and sandwiches, but seemed unable to move out of the shelter and seek further help.

He'd totally withdrawn into himself and I guessed he'd had a mental breakdown or an ASD, or both. I and some friends from Eastbourne District General Hospital, where I was doing my nurse training, befriended him, as far as he'd allow us to get close to him – relationally, I mean. Getting close to him physically was also a problem. He was ashamed of the terrible stench emanating from his feet, and was only ever able to take a few steps within the shelter. We never did find out was wrong with his feet, despite our offers to look at them and see if we could help medically in some way. The shame, or fear of whatever might be found, was too much for him to ever remove those boots, however hard we tried to persuade him.

One day we heard that he'd died and that his boots had been full of maggots. What killed him, we never knew. His death seemed inevitable, but we were still heartbroken. And we never did get to hear the story behind his destitution.

* * *

Ridicule, whether through unjust cardboard labels or class mockery, as well as stunting educational growth, also breeds shame.

Since faith in Jesus emerged miraculously in my life, I've experienced incredible shame-busting forgiveness in stages, and the boundlessness of the utter compassion of God grows and grows in my vision. The sense of "naughtiness" should have gone forever.

In fact, I believe wholeheartedly that the day I first prayed a few simple words of faith, when God entered into my life, is somehow, mystically, tied in with the day that Jesus lovingly gave up his life on a cross for total forgiveness and healing for all – it's as if they were the same day – because time is irrelevant to Yahweh[15], the ageless, eternal One.

I believe wholeheartedly that from the day I found simple faith in Jesus, my life was entirely forgiven, my being totally absorbed into the being of Yahweh, who is love...

– and that the reality of that truth is

even bigger

than my experience
of transformational change.

And yet, if I'm honest, I'd say that I still struggle to *completely* shake off a fear of being "bad" and subconsciously try to prove my worth by my actions. But I'm learning.

Issues of self-esteem, like any other ingrained psychological pattern, are for many people never entirely resolved.

---

[15] Yahweh, meaning 'I Am' – the name God identifies himself as to Moses and the ancient Hebrews.

People like me can become workaholics, driven to succeed, to atone for sins that no longer need atoning for. No doubt one of the reasons many recovering alcoholics become *work*aholics.

The title of Lansbury's book referred to above, *No Bad Kids*, may sit uncomfortably with certain schools of Christian thought, who preach that we're born sinners, but my theology after 30 years as a Christian has grown to emphasise the "original goodness" of man over "original sin". From a Biblical perspective, goodness precedes sin; i.e. those allegorical figures representing humankind, Adam and Eve, were created good before they became "bad".

It's probably that inner sense of false guilt that's driven me to emphasise repeatedly – in my blog and in this book – about man's essential goodness, in a drive to convince myself as much as others.

How we turn out is a mix of genetics, cultural conditioning, life experiences and personal choices, and to what extent each of these elements plays its part is the subject of much philosophical debate. There seems to be a very good case, though, for the idea that personal choice has but a bit part in this play of life.

Having worked with vulnerable, chaotic and homeless individuals with their offending histories, drug addictions, alcoholism and mental health disorders for a number of years, and being privileged to receive insight into many life stories, as I've grown in my understanding of the chain reactions that have formed the persons that they are, and as my theology of God's compassion constantly expands like the universe he's made.... I tend increasingly towards the view that these individuals had virtually *no* control over the way their adult lives have developed.

A homeless man whose own mother tried to drown him when he was a child.

A man in his 30s, born an addict to a drug-addicted mother, serving several years in prison for stabbing his girlfriend.

A woman constantly selling her body for sex, who was passed from pillar to post as a child in foster care and never knew the stabilising influence of a father's or mother's unconditional love.

Early abuse or trauma setting off an inevitable chain reaction.

What chance have they had?

I have 2 favourite films: *Airplane* (it's a big flying machine with wings but that's not important right now[16]) and *Good Will Hunting*. If you haven't seen *Good Will Hunting*, go and watch it now, then come back and carry on reading this book...

I'll wait...

...

...

...

...

...

...

...

...

...

...

...

---

[16] If you've watched Airplane, you'll get this. If you haven't, you need to. Seriously.

So you've watched the film now?

You haven't? OK, then I'll explain...

The central character, Will Hunting, played brilliantly by Matt Damon, is a tearaway youth who grew up with an abusive foster father, and who turns out to be a mathematical genius, but rejects all career, counselling and romantic opportunities that come his way because all he's ever known is failure, rejection and struggle. He remains locked up in his world of fatalistic pessimism and rage.

To help unlock that mathematical talent, the professor who discovers his genius offers him psychotherapy with a succession of colleagues, all of whom give up in exasperation at Will's defiant mind games, until the maverick Dr Sean Maguire, played equally brilliantly by the late great Robin Williams, comes along and identifies with him, persisting through Will's attempts to repel him.

The pivotal turning-point in the film comes when Sean looks at Will and pronounces with serious, almost severe, sincerity:

"It's not your fault."

"Yeah, I know," mumbles Will, casually, from across the room.

"It's not your fault," reiterates Sean.

Will becomes increasingly uncomfortable and agitated as his tough exterior starts to melt away and Sean gradually closes in on Will's personal space, declaring repeatedly:

"It's not your fault."

"Don't fuck with me, Sean."

"It's not your fault," Sean persists, moving closer, unflinchingly pressing his point.

Will's defences are gradually demolished until he breaks down and sobs on his counsellor's shoulder.

It's the most moving scene ever. I can barely hold back the tears myself whenever I watch it.

The message sinks in. The penny drops.

Will no longer needs to carry the burden of shame and guilt for the person he's become, and he's now free to be everything he was always intended to be.

I so relate to that. Jesus says to me, and to all who come to him: "I absorb all your guilt and shame, whether you're to blame or not. I took it all at the cross, so you can be free to be everything you were always intended to be."

Love that.

* * *

At age 13 I took a scholarship exam for Ardingly College, a mediocre public school in the heart of the Sussex countryside, and won their second-top scholarship – again, on the strength of just two or three subjects – meaning a significant reduction in fees and making it possible for my parents to send me there.

Once again, expectations were high.

I did OK. Being closeted away in boarding school, away from too many distractions, and with dedicated "prep" (homework) time, I managed to pass enough O-levels to get by, achieving A-grades in Maths and French a year early, and scraping by in a few others: all languages, nothing else.

But on returning to school after a several-week suspension for selling stolen goods to the kids, I was named and shamed in morning assembly where it was made clear that better things were expected of a scholarship pupil.

Shoplifting had become quite a habit by early- to mid-teens. I was quite skilled at it and got away with hundreds of pounds worth of theft, but also so prolific and took so many risks, that getting caught became quite a regular occurrence as well. Some shops would just let me off with a warning; other shopkeepers would contact my parents. Huge shame was involved.

Funnily enough, this was the one time I received a Junior Criminal Record – when I hadn't actually been caught red-handed. I discovered I could nick Scalextric cars easily from a shop in nearby Haywards Heath and sell them on to kids at school who had these racing car sets. It was quite a lucrative line of business, until unfortunately for me someone snitched to a prefect, who snitched to a teacher, who inevitably informed my parents and the police.

Hence the suspension from school.

As a Magistrates Clerk, a lawyer who advised Magistrates on court cases, my Dad was known and respected professionally by the local police force, so it was with great embarrassment that he accompanied me to a local police station to be issued with the JCR.

Shame all round. Expectations shattered.

Apart from the shoplifting incident, there was my ongoing struggle with concepts involved in reading and analysing material. Unfortunately, many of the subjects I was good at – languages – involved a lot of literature, which I couldn't get my head round – one of the reasons I just about did OK at O-levels and gave up on A-levels.

The other reason for flunking A-levels was my new-found freedom in the transition from boarding school to comprehensive sixth form. Freedom, friends, and girls.

I mean, given the choice between trying to wrestle with a German literature text book and playing cards with the best friends you've ever had while listening to the record player in the common room – there's no contest, is there?

Especially when there seems to be no future worth striving for.

My two years at Lewes Priory Sixth Form were some of the best days of my life, in all kinds of ways. Several of the friendships formed then have stood the test of time, renewed partly by the magic of social media. I'm so grateful for beautiful people like Madcat Alan, Nancy, Dave B, Andrea, Nancy's brother David, and others, for whom I have huge affection, and for the sweet reunions we've had in recent years.

How miraculous, also, that Nancy and Andrea now share my faith, making those friendships and reunions deeper and sweeter than ever. Some friendships were just meant to be.

At Priory we played endless hours of Knockout Whist, Bridge, Black Mariah and Cheat in the common room, and at weekends enjoyed – or endured – gruelling pub crawls, joyfully singing The House of the Rising Sun down the middle of Lewes high street. Teenage stupidity? Or friends bonding for life?

I came away with a D in French. The other exams I failed or just didn't bother to turn up for.

Do I regret flunking A-levels?

Not really. Things are what they are. I had no motivation or mindset to be any other way at the time.

Also, I'm grateful for the 2 years I spent at Ardingly where, despite the problems and the constantly cruel atmosphere of verbal bullying, of which I was both perpetrator and victim, I came away with enough O-levels, including the mandatory Maths, to enter nursing a few years later when my life turned upside-down and inside-out and I embarked on a career I've never looked back on.

5: Give us this day our daily bread and Marmite

Biblical prayer is impertinent, persistent, shameless, indecorous. It is more like haggling in an outdoor bazaar than the polite monologues of the church.
Walter Wink

At school, the Lord's Prayer was a dry, daily, religious ritual in morning assembly that was never given any explanation. Perhaps it was an atheist conspiracy designed to put us all off Christianity, religion and Jesus, for *life*. Probably not, but if it had been, it very nearly worked.

There was one particular assembly when Martin and I improvised this daily drudgery. When we got to "Give us this day our daily bread...", we continued: "...and Marmite and jam and honey and chocolate spread..." and carried on going, giggling, as long as we could think of more spreads and foods that would go nicely with bread.

As silly 9- or 10-year-olds, it all seemed highly amusing. Unfortunately, the snotty prefect (who I won't name and shame, even though I do remember his name!) who heard us giggling but didn't hear *what* we were saying, *didn't* find us amusing. He reported us to the headmaster for "talking during the Lord's Prayer".

Sacrilege! Blasphemy!

The head was known as JR. When the infamous baddie JR Ewing later swaggered on to our TV screens in the new soap opera *Dallas* in the late '70s, we all knew at school that JR Ewing would never be any match for JR

Ward – that our JR was far badder and scarier than JR Ewing. No one crossed JR Ward.

So it was with trepidation that we were made to wait outside JR's office of doom and gloom – a room that smelt of fusty furniture and irrefutable Authority – wondering what his verdict would be. I'm sure he deliberately kept us waiting as long as possible, to make us *sweat*.

As it turned out, he had the sense not to do much at all. We were given a mild reprimand, and that was it. I'd like to think the snotty prefect was also rebuked for wasting JR's time!

On reflection, our pure and innocent silliness could equally have been a great prayer, giving thanks for all the choice and variety on offer to have with our bread. The Bible says frequently to give thanks for *every* good thing. I think now that my Father smiled with Martin and me over that "prayer".

But nothing in childhood did anything to make me think there was a God. In fact, I was about 5 when I decided I didn't believe in God. I'm not really sure why, but here are some possible events that led to my atheism...

My parents took us to church occasionally and, I guess, Christianity was more a part of our culture's everyday vocabulary back then, so whether to believe in God was a question to be asked and answered, one way or the other, whereas perhaps today, for a lot of people, it's not necessarily even a question to be considered.

My Dad had been a Christian until a few years before I was born, when the trauma of losing his first wife had left him feeling that God had abandoned him – or had never been there in the first place.

By the time he met his second wife, Simone, my Mum-to-be, a couple of years later, church and God had slipped into the sidelines, not quite altogether forgotten. And so, we had the occasional visit to a C of E church in nearby Uckfield – stony experiences in a stony church, that probably did more to inoculate me against faith than draw me towards it. Those visits finally stopped and my Dad continued on an upright, secular, agnostic / atheist path, Sunday mornings now filled with playing tennis rather than worshipping God.

Like a lot of people with a religious background, he retained a strong sense of morality, but without the spiritual dynamic of faith to empower and guide his life.

As the years went by, it gradually became clearer that there was no future to aim for, my mindset presumably shaped by the unhappiness I witnessed in my parents' participation in the rat race, combined with my struggles at school and a belief that nothing ultimately mattered. Future was futile.

During Sixth Form I submitted an article to the school magazine on the meaninglessness of life, in which I cited Sex Pistols bassist Sid Vicious as a hero to be emulated because he seemed to live as a true anarchist who didn't care about tomorrow or what anyone else thought.

In later years I came to realise that Sid was sadly more of a messed-up heroin addict, manipulated by Malcolm McLaren and the media, than any kind of working-class hero or role model, and that if anyone deserved to be idolised, it was his less media-minded, more reflective bandmate Johnny Rotten, aka John Lydon. What was not as obvious in punk's heyday as it is now, is that Lydon is and was a stickler for integrity and honesty, a champion of fairness.

Interestingly, there's a radio interview from 1978 that was doing the rounds on the internet, in which Lydon / Rotten discusses a list of people he'd like to kill, including Jimmy Savile, whom he brands a "hypocrite". He makes insinuations about Savile which, he says, "we're not allowed to talk about." The interview was originally hidden from the public's ears during the great BBC cover-up of the late '70s. Lydon was vilified by the BBC and the rest of the media for his raucous genuineness, while Savile and others, on account of their celebrity status, were treated as irreproachable with entitlement to go on abusing and destroying the lives of children and young people.

Lydon reminds me of some of the ordinary people in the Bible who are commended for speaking their mind, even when their comments may seem offensive – like Nathanael who, when he first heard about Jesus of Nazareth, asked the derogatory rhetorical question, "Can anything good come from Nazareth?" Jesus was fine about Nathanael dissing both him and his home town in this one smart remark, even describing him as "a genuine son of Israel – a man of complete integrity."

Free speech and real opinions are Christian values, despite any evidence to the contrary.

In the essay for the school magazine I referred to Christians and other people of faith as "religious nutters" who needed a crutch to lean on. Probably not very PC, even back then, but at least I was being genuine! Maybe that's why they didn't publish it. I was disappointed, though – my ideas didn't fit into the narrow agenda that the students who ran the magazine seemed to have.

Such was my view of a meaningless universe.

Another expression of this sense of futility, around that time, was a plan to commit suicide. I wasn't depressed or even feeling particularly down. It just seemed absolutely pointless to go through all the hassles of living life in this world, so why bother? The plan involved a knife, a bottle of whisky and some tablets. I had it worked out in my head, although I was never really sure I would have actually gone through with it.

The meaninglessness of life as I perceived it was perhaps a pretty weak basis for a suicide plan – hence it didn't take a lot for me to change my mind. When it came to my attention that my sister's friend's sister fancied me, the possibility of a girlfriend was enough to steer me back towards living! Plan cancelled.

The instinctive drive to preserve life is pretty strong.

The third clear symptom of this atheism and belief that nothing ultimately mattered was a descending morality – in fact, a leaning towards *amorality*. If this universe is ultimately pointless, what's the point of ethics? Of course, I did have morals. I wouldn't steal off my friends, although I had repeatedly stolen from family. Deep inside us all, whatever we believe about life, there seems to be an innate sense of being part of a community, of our actions being part of a wider context than just our own life.

That considered (but entirely selfish) rejection of morality expressed itself in a number of ways – sexually, relationally, and in my treatment of other people generally – particularly in the year or two before faith in Jesus moved into my life like a weird but welcome new kid on the block.

I was quite a serious atheist. Not a fanatical or militant one like Dawkins or the late Hitchens, out to convert anyone with even the vaguest belief in God to atheism, but serious in my own adamant expression of it. Like the time I declared my atheism to my grandmother.

Nanny was the sweetest grandmother ever. Yes, I know everyone thinks their gran is the best, but she *really was*. And don't argue!

My grandparents lived in Holland and we'd visit maybe once a year, often at Christmas. Records were much cheaper there than in the UK, and the first LP I ever bought, as a recent convert to punk, was the Sex Pistols' *Never Mind the Bollocks*[17], in a record shop round the corner from where my grandparents lived.

On my return to their flat, Nanny, taking an interest in my record, insisted ever so sweetly that I put it on their record player. Despite my very best efforts to dissuade her from this disastrous idea – "No, Nanny, you *really* wouldn't like it" – her persistence won through. As the first track, *Holidays in the Sun*, thundered out into the room, Nanny smiled kindly at the music she couldn't possibly have liked: "It's nice, it's nice!" – such was her sweet grace.

My grandmother, a Catholic, would say grace before meals. At one family mealtime in Holland, I defiantly desisted from taking part in grace. Eyes open, arms folded. When Nanny questioned me about it, I explained, "I don't believe in God."

Her response was, "But you *must* believe in God."

Not in a mandatory tone of: "You HAVE TO believe in God!"

More a bemused "How can you *not* believe in God?"

I don't remember any other conversations between us about God or religion, but I think that single exchange left a deep impression on me and a respect for Nanny's faith.

So much so that, some years later, when a miracle of new life had exploded within me from atheist to Christian, one of the first things I did was to write to her, informing her of my newfound faith.

---

[17] Sex Pistols, *Never Mind the Bollocks Here's the Sex Pistols* (album), Virgin Records, 1977.

The letter I received back from her (dated 22nd Feb '88, below) remains one of my most treasured possessions.

Here are some excerpts from the letter from my grandmother:

"When you went to America, I was worried about you. The only thing I could do was to pray and asked the good Lord to protect you. I was so pleased to hear that you were back safely and thanked God!

...and you must believe me, there is a good Hand who leads you."

Later chapters of this book reveal more about how Nanny's prayers were amazingly answered in America. I'm so grateful for her love, faith and prayers, which helped to pave the way for the life I have now.

As a practising Catholic, I'll bet she also prayed the Lord's Prayer.

***

For years after coming to faith, I couldn't recite the Lord's Prayer with others in church – I'd keep silent. The prayer just reminded me of dull, meaningless school religion. I've moved on since then, and participate now, happily and meaningfully.

In fact I've come to love and treasure the Lord's Prayer. It serves as a sequence of themes emanating from God's heart that guide me as I pray, starting from a springboard of meditation on the compassionate fatherhood of God: Our Father in heaven...

I also try and remember to keep thanking God for all the little things in life, like bread and Marmite and jam and honey and chocolate spread.

6: Psychotic or mystic?

In the night that settles

like snow over the city,

a blanket to smother the day,

while under the silence

those for whom sleep is no shelter

struggle to settle their souls,

God calls to us.

Gerard Kelly – *The Call*[18]

CAUTION AHEAD! STOP! WRONG WAY! DEAD END!

Bruce is oblivious to the road signs flashing in front of his eyes, as he careers distractedly down the highway, pleading desperately with God for a signal, a sign, some guidance, a miracle, anything...

He crashes the car. Of course he blames it on God. Eventually, though, Bruce (Jim Carrey) kneels on the highway in surrender to God, and in so doing is hit by a truck and killed! As you do...

Morgan Freeman, I mean God, sees the bigger picture and uses all Bruce's circumstances for the greater good. Bruce is defibrillated back to life – to start living again with a new purpose.

But how did Bruce fail to see the signs?

And does God speak to people who are angry with him? Or even to atheists?

---

[18] Gerard Kelly, Spoken Worship: *Living Words for Personal and Public Prayer* (Grand Rapids: Zondervan, 2007).

Does God believe in people who don't believe in him?!

Could it be that there are non-religious people missing signs that God is giving them?

And how does the film *Bruce Almighty* manage to address so many profound questions so brilliantly???!

***

I only recently realised that not everyone lives their lives through song lyrics. You may have noticed already that there are a lot of songs cited in this book, and there are plenty more to come.

Unfortunately I discovered (or fortunately I discovered in time) that gaining permission from record companies to quote song lyrics directly is costly, and quoting more than 4-5 words of a song *without* permission could turn out to be even costlier! *Titles*, however, aren't copyrighted, hence the references to songs throughout this book, without any direct lyric quotations longer than a few words.

Apparently, other people just enjoy music for music's sake, while a few people – dreamers or romantics, maybe – find meaning in the words.

Is it just me?

But supposing something in our subconscious recognises in a song or film or book some message that we're "*meant*" to hear, but we choose to ignore it?

Or supposing we've become desensitised to this whole idea by our busy, secular culture?

Could there be messages out there for us in songs, films, books, dreams, billboards... messages that we're meant to hear, at just the right time, for particular situations? Supposing the Universe – or God, even – is trying to communicate with us, for our own good? Supposing there's a force for good in this world that wants to speak to us?

Some would call that spirituality, or even mysticism. Others, like Richard Dawkins, might call it psychosis. In the past, such mystics were called witches and burned at the stake. Today in the West, they might just be crucified in print.

As someone close to me said years ago, perhaps I just read too much into things.

But could it be that God does in fact speak, even to atheists?

***

My second attempt to escape from society as we know it came in 1987, at the age of 19. After the lost-in-London escapade, I continued through the motions of A-Levels, even turning up to half of the exams, having the time of my life with the best friends I've ever had, as mentioned earlier, until... School came to an end, and those friends dispersed to universities and far-flung places, leaving this lost soul more alone than ever before.

For me, Alice Cooper's rallying cry *School's Out*[19] turned out to be a huge anti-climax rather than cause for celebration. I had more freedom and fun at sixth form than I'd ever had before.

My sister had prudently chosen to flee the tense family nest two years earlier, to pursue a gap year, then Uni. My parents finally divorced, and I was left living alone with Dad. We had lost any real relationship with each other many years earlier. For a long time we'd been at loggerheads, and now the friction came to a head:

---

[19] Alice Cooper, *School's Out*, Warner Bros, 1972.

- me in my disaffected teenage angst and arrogance, my soul tattered by years of domestic turbulence, in a state of psychological and spiritual rootlessness, and in my self-centred world, entirely blind to the problems faced by Dad or anyone else;
- my Dad going through his own trauma of a broken marriage, while trying to manage an intensely demanding professional job; this stressful state of being no doubt exacerbating his delusion that he was always right;
- both of us challenged more than we knew by our disintegrating lives, without the skills or opportunity to express our pain, least of all to each other.

There was one occasion during that period, though, when I felt compassion for him.

If you're as old as me, you'll probably remember that in 1984, during the Frankie Goes to Hollywood phenomenon, there were T-shirts everywhere proclaiming "FRANKIE SAYS RELAX", "FRANKIE SAYS THIS" and "FRANKIE SAYS THAT".

Well, I'd managed to find a T-shirt in a little shop in Brighton that protested, "FUCK WHAT FRANKIE SAYS"! It was brilliant. When I turned up to punk gigs wearing it, people laughed and said "Love the T-shirt!"

Of course, I never let my Dad see it, but one day he came across the garment in my wardrobe and was most upset. My Dad, whose name was Frank, thought I'd had the T-shirt specially printed as a protest against *him*. I was genuinely sorry that he could have thought this, and had to explain to him about Frankie Goes to Hollywood.

Maybe there's a lesson to us parents there about staying in touch with the culture of our kids' generation! I mean, how could my poor, longsuffering Dad have missed the FGTH / Relax trend and misunderstood what the T-shirt was all about?

***

In my state of loneliness, existential aloneness and difficulties at home, I ambled through dead-end jobs.

My first job as forecourt attendant and car valet at a garage in Uckfield, was actually quite enjoyable, serving petrol and transforming ramshackle used cars to gleaming, like-new models fit for the garage owner to sell to any gullible (I mean, prospective) customer.

In my trusted position working alone at weekends, I'd often steal cash out of the till, by not ringing up some of the petrol sales, so at the end of the day the till still balanced. As I was never caught and never seemed to raise any suspicions, I was given a glowing reference by the owner when I left. Many years later, in my amends-making, I sent a cheque with a letter of admission and apology to him, but the cheque was never cashed, so I guess it never reached him. Maybe he'd moved. I wished the cheque had got there, but in making reparations we can only be responsible for our efforts, not for the results.

After over a year working in the petrol station, I moved to a job at Martin's the newsagent, in Lewes, in early '85, for a change and for slightly better money. For all of about 6 weeks I turned up each day in a shirt and tie, served on the tills and checked stock levels, tortured by the awful mid-'80s records and tapes that were sold and played in the shop. I missed working outdoors and the relative rough-'n'-readiness of the garage. Martin's turned out to be the most mindless, sanitised job I've ever had the misfortune to end up in. Not that I'd decry anyone else for working in retail; it just wasn't for me.

It was into this barren, dead-end landscape of my lifeless life, devoid of real family, friendship, fulfilment or any sense of future, that adventure came rolling in once again like a luxury limo, this time in the form of a female.

And the road beckoned again.

***

I met Helen in France. I'd travelled over there to visit my sister, Ruth. Helen was studying at Dundee University and, like Ruth, was spending a year in France as part of her degree. We had a whirlwind romance. Helen was something of a free spirit and, like me, had a taste for adventure. We discovered lots in common, and fell in love.

So much so that, a few weeks later, Helen made the journey over to England to see me. We met up at the end of my Friday shift at Martin's, shared some vodka and made plans to spend a weekend camping together.

One of the chart songs being played with annoying frequency in Martin's in 1985, was Philip Bailey and Phil Collins' No.1 hit *Easy Lover*[20]. Much as I disliked the music of Phil Collins (sorry, Phil)...there was something else... The song *Easy Lover bothered* me.

Not only was I unreligious, I had no sense of spirituality and I mocked superstition. I'd deliberately walk under ladders. I had no belief in fate, karma, God, heaven, hell, or soul. This world, and what we can see, was it.

---

[20] Philip Bailey and Phil Collins, Easy *Lover*, Columbia, 1984.

And yet, it was as if *something* was giving me a warning about this relationship that I'd thrown myself headlong into. Not that I ever properly articulated this thought, even in my head, but there was a subconscious, foreboding feeling, through the words of the song, about the inevitable end result of this romance.

To be fair, both of us had fallen easily into this thing. We were both, in a sense, easy lovers.

Perhaps, despite my emotional illiteracy, there was an intuitive self-awareness that, especially when it came to women, my disconnectedness made me liable to dependency, infatuation and therefore, ultimately, rejection.

But young love, mingled with obsession and teenage lust, is blind to inevitable futures.

Could it be that God speaks to atheists through dreams or even...mediocre mid-'80s chart songs? Who knows?

And if God was trying to communicate with me, would he have expected the messed-up, mangled teenager that was me to listen and respond? Probably not.

But as a friend of mine said once, when we were discussing the ways God works mysteriously in this world: "We don't know the half of it!"

***

Helen and I had planned to camp together somewhere for the weekend. First, though, we took my 2-person tent and spent a night pitched in a park in Lewes, where the police looked in on us and informed us we weren't strictly allowed to camp there, but decided to leave us alone.

Again, no word from me to my Dad about where I was. Sadly, I was too immature, and my relationship with him too broken, for me to have any thought for him or his feelings.

But within 24 hours, our plans to go camping somewhere further afield had turned into a mad plan to "elope" to America.

We worked out what we'd need to do:

1. Hitch-hike from Lewes to Uckfield to withdraw the few hundred quid my parents had saved in a building society account for me since I was little and had recently given me independent access to;

2. Pick up my passport, rucksack and other bits & bobs from home in Buxted;

3. Hitch-hike up to London to obtain visas from the American Embassy;

4. Then hitch to Gatwick to catch the cheapest single flight to New York.

It started as a joke, a *hypothetical* strategy: what would we need to do *if* we eloped to America?

Again, there was nothing to lose, certainly from my point-of-view, and we impetuously started acting out the reckless plan, not even sure we really intended to carry it out:

1. Money drawn out from building society and exchanged for travellers cheques and dollars – check.

2. Passport and other bits & bobs picked up from home – check.

3. Hitched to London; visas granted – check.

4. Hitched to Gatwick; 2 single tickets to Newark, New Jersey, purchased – check!

Within 4 days of having met back up in Lewes, we'd gone from having an idea about escaping to America, to actually sitting on a plane to the USA, enjoying Virgin Atlantic hospitality. Astounded at our own audacity as we sat on those plane seats during take-off, we looked at each other and laughed, and one of us summed up our crazy situation well with the rhetorical question: "What the fuck are we doing?!"

Born out of an otherwise hopeless situation, it was the most wild, impulsive thing I've ever done. Probably more impulsive than anything most people ever do.

Somewhere in the midst of those 4 days, we also hitched to Surrey University in Guildford to visit Dave B and stayed a night with him. Dave was the *only* person who knew what we were doing until after we'd left. Once again, my poor Dad had to report me as a missing person. The manager and staff at Martin's had no idea where I was when I failed to turn up for work on Monday morning. Not even any of my other friends knew a thing about it.

The only other attempt I made at communication was a postcard I sent with a resentful message to Dad from Gatwick Airport, which didn't arrive till a whole week later. I'm not sure even now how or when the news of my escape with Helen reached his ears, only that he had several days' worry, with not a clue as to where I was or what had happened to me.

As described in Stiff Little Fingers' *At the Edge*[21], which had played repeatedly on my record player in the me-world of my bedroom, home was somewhere I'd given up believing in, despite providing everything I

---

[21] Stiff Little Fingers, *At The Edge*, Chrysalis, 1980.

supposedly needed. Such was the sentiment behind the postcard to my Dad.

***

Although there was a fair amount of American TV on British screens even then, I was unprepared for how different the USA was from England, how different from how I might have imagined it. Helen and I were both quite naive. For a start, we thought we could just stroll into America… Immigration officials at Newark Airport looked with suspicion at these 2 long-haired youths with our bulky rucksacks, sleeping bags and single plane tickets. According to them, the money we had with us, taking into account their expectation for us to buy flight tickets home, was enough for us to live on for 2 weeks.

Our plan was to live on the ludicrous pittance of $5/day, make our money last for months, and get some casual, cash-in-hand work along the way. We were going to travel the States for a few years, at least.

They eventually stamped our passports, reluctantly letting us into their beloved country for a whole 2 weeks.

In hindsight, especially with our single tickets, I'm surprised they let us in at all. But our plan to stay for years was in no way dampened by our brush with US Immigration.

By this time it was late at night, so we pitched our tent on a patch of grass between the roads right outside the airport. The next surprise, on emerging from the tent in the morning, was just how warm it was. I had no idea it was generally hotter in the States than in the UK. This was April, and on our first day's hitch-hiking I went shirtless and got burnt.

Like Jo-Jo[22], I'd left home in search of – amongst other things – some California grass. Our goal was California, but we were in no rush and,

61

while we were in New Jersey, decided to head for Atlantic City to sample the glitzy lights and gambling.

On our way there, however, we hitched a ride with a young couple who treated us to some good food, cocaine, and not California but New Jersey grass. On our first day in the USA we had our first taste of American hospitality, and our first taste of cocaine. I laughed like I'd never laughed before at whatever was on telly. Mindless US TV had never been so funny. I suppose it's not surprising that I can't remember why we never made it to Atlantic City. All I know is that it took us a few months and several thousand miles of hitching in zig-zag directions to finally reach California. As I said, we were in no hurry.

The next major event, all of a few days later, was hitching our first ride with a truck driver – Rick – out of Pittsburgh, Pennsylvania. Over a period of a few days he took us more than 2000 miles, staying in motels along the way, up to Ohio (right up in the north), where he was picking up a load, all the way down to the searing heat of Austin, Texas, to drop off the load, then finally to his house in Arkansas where we met his family, stayed in his caravan next to the house for a few days, and sampled some good ol' US country hospitality.

That week I learned that truck drivers don't walk anywhere unless they have to, that Arkansas isn't pronounced how it looks, and more about country music than I'd ever wanted to know. By the time I left America, I even learned to appreciate some country – if you can't beat 'em, join 'em – but it took that long.

---

[22] In The Beatles, *Get Back*, Apple, 1969.

That scene in Blues Brothers, where the bar owners boast with blissful ignorance that they play *both* kinds of music – Country *and* Western – was not far from the reality of many of the truck drivers and other US folk we hitched rides with.

The zigzaggy hitch-hiking was partly the result of accepting lifts pretty much to wherever people were going, as long as it was vaguely west – with the emphasis on *vaguely*.

Which is why we ended up in Denver, Colorado, working for and living with a painter-decorator, for about 6 weeks.

It was a strange arrangement. Charlie let us sleep on the water-bed in his bedroom, the floor of which was piled high with porn magazines, while he slept in a spare room. I think perhaps he only took us on because he fancied his chances with Helen. Or maybe, he found us curious, I don't know. Lots of Americans treated us with great curiosity, asking what we eat in England, whether we'd ever met Princess Diana or Boy George (some of these inquisitors seemed to be under the impression that England was a tiny village), and even what *language* we speak in England! Go figure...

Nevertheless, Charlie kindly gave us free board & lodging and cash-in-hand for basic labouring work, which set us up financially to keep us going for a good while longer.

Colorado also treated us to the magic of the Rocky Mountains, bejewelled with flashes of hummingbirds and the comforting aroma of pine forests. There in the Rockies, we somehow got a few days work with two crazed loggers (US) / lumberjacks (UK) called Dan and Don, who drunkenly crashed pick-up trucks and brought down giant trees. I can't actually remember their names; but most of the men we met seemed to be called Dan or Don.

But we were finding Colorado too hot as the summer wore on, so decided to head northwest to Washington state, which we were told was temperate, "like England". Little did we know that Washington was experiencing a heatwave at the time, hotter than Colorado.

The day we arrived in some small Washington town, the high street was deserted, like a ghost town in an old western movie. One of those illuminated temperature displays on the side of a building silently screamed 100⁰ F (37⁰ C). Like everyone else, we took shelter inside, spending the rest of the afternoon drinking coffee in the cool, cool air conditioning of the first restaurant we could find, until it looked like we were going to get chucked out for loitering.

I developed my coffee habit in the States – before coffee was a thing in England. Everywhere did free filter coffee refills in the States – even McDonald's, if I remember rightly. Apparently they still do. Why don't they do that here in England? You see, there *are* things we can learn from America!

We next escaped the heat by making it over to the Hoh Rainforest, situated on the Olympic Peninsula, in the very northwest tip of mainland America. With its multi-verdant-shades of overhanging vines constantly dripping wetness, Hoh boasts being the most northerly rainforest in the world. When we got to Hoh, it was raining. And then it rained. Then rained some more. Maybe that's why they call it a rainforest.

We endured about 2 days and nights, trapped in our tent, trying to keep ourselves and the inside of the tent dry, before we got stir crazy and had to leave.

Puget Sound, still in Washington, was our next port of call – a beautiful stretch of water in sight of the snow-capped Mount Rainier, surrounded by shady pine forests where, unusually, we camped in an actual campsite for a few days.

Out in front of us sat a small, inviting island just asking to be swum to. I was a late learner when it came to swimming, and I'd only recently learned to manage more than about a length; yet the distance to the far-off island somehow looked do-able. Once we got out into the water, it seemed further than we first thought; but we kept on going, convinced we could make it. And after a very long effort, completely exhausted and longing to touch down on shore, we did.

However, once we got there, we discovered the shore was one razor-sharp mass of barnacles, impossible to stand on. We couldn't get on to the island and were too tired to swim back, so we were in effect *stuck*, able only to tread water.

And the only reason I tell this story is because I like to brag about all the different modes of transport I've ever managed to hitch-hike on and this is the one time I hitched a ride on a boat. Moored next to the island was a luxury yacht, whose owners, much to our relief, took pity on us, welcomed us on board and sailed us back to mainland.

***

On we headed towards California. But there was one big thing that stood between us and California – the state of Oregon.

Oregon, Oregon, what special memories I have of you, Oregon (more to follow later).

Months earlier, we'd hitched a ride with a truck driver, Carl, who'd given us his address in Portland. We took up his offer to go and visit, and stayed with his wife Sarah, and their 2 teenage sons, Joel and Mikey. Most of the time we stayed there, Carl was out on the road, but like many Americans we met, the Edelmans showed us incredible warmth and hospitality.

Also in Oregon, in a typical seaside town called...Seaside, an older man called Ed put us up and gave us some work painting & decorating his home, again financing us for further adventures. Oregon had treated us kindly on our way to the Sunshine State.

Our introduction to California involved an encounter with a small town fittingly named Eureka, which we entered via coastal Highway 101 in a beat-up old hippy car driven by a beat-up old hippy, with *Let It Be*, the album, playing on his cassette player.

It was the first time I'd heard the Beatles' *Two of Us*[23] – and it seemed the perfect accompaniment to our stoned trip south into California, as Lennon and McCartney's voices filled the car, celebrating being on their way home.

Having no real home, heading for California with its promises of sunshine and happiness stretched out ahead of us was "as good as". This was living the dream – again.

We were dropped off in Eureka, where we ended up following Doc, a homeless man in his 50s or 60s with long, flowing white hair and – I suspect – a mental health disorder that had alienated him from society. I guess "Doc" wasn't his real name. Isn't it curious how street people tend to adopt nicknames, often based on some distinguishing feature or the place they're from? Maybe it's because surnames are too "official", associated with the police and "the system". Friends don't need to know

---

[23] The Beatles, *Two of Us*, from the album *Let It Be*, Apple, 1970.

your surname. So if there are 2 Bobs or Billys amongst a town's street community, they have nicknames rather than surnames to distinguish them.

Some ten years later, in the 90s, I found myself living in South-East London, running a Saturday morning drop-in for our local homeless community (more on this later), where we got to know a Scottish gentleman called 28p Jonny.

Jonny had a cheeky, cheerful smile. I have a charming black-and-white photo I took of Jonny, his laughing face short on teeth but full of life and his arm round Alistair, one of the drop-in volunteers. In the photo, Alistair looks understandably a little taken aback, but mostly returning the love. His speech frequently incoherent to us Southerners who were poorly trained in discerning that challenging mix of Glasgow and alcohol, Jonny would often speak of "my Father" with a faraway glint of faith in his eye, like he knew something personal only to him.

Despite his homelessness, he seemed to know the genuine happiness of resting in the Father's love.

One cold evening in March 1996, walking home with Janine from our first ever date, we came across Jonny lying on the pavement on Hither Green Lane, battling against the late winter temperatures, trying to sleep. We had a chat, then after popping over to Janine's flat, returned with a sleeping-bag – an auspicious encounter that seemed to help seal Janine's and my future life together. Thank you, 28p Jonny, we're forever indebted to you for this legacy.

Jonny would sit on the pavement in Hither Green, asking passers-by for 28p, hence the nickname. One day someone explained to us the reason for this strange request: apparently 4 x 28p (£1.12) equalled the price of a can of Tennent's Extra.

So *that* was why he was known as 28p Jonny!

Like too many homeless people I've known, one day we heard that he had suddenly died. We never did hear the cause of death. Perhaps it was alcohol-related; perhaps he'd been assaulted or suffered one of the many other problems associated with the vulnerability of living on the streets. Reliable research into the mortality of homeless people has put the average age of death of male rough sleepers in England as 47, and even younger (43) for homeless women – some 30 years lower than the general population.[24]

Amongst the street community, people find a family, an alternative community, and a new identity. In my second trip round the States, in '87, when I merged for a while into the street community (as you'll read about later), I was told by a homeless guy in Mississippi that I needed a nickname. He came up with "Hap", short for "Happy". He seemed to think that's what I was. I liked "Hap" but thought it should stand for "Haphazard".

I love the fact that Jesus, who had his own little street community, gave his friends nicknames. Jewish society at that time didn't really do surnames, so they needed something to distinguish them, especially if they had popular names like James and John, two brothers who followed

[24] Crisis, *Homelessness Kills: An analysis of the mortality of homeless people in early twenty-first century England* (London: Crisis, 2012).
https://www.crisis.org.uk/media/236799/crisis_homelessness_kills_es2012.pdf

Jesus. Jesus called them "Sons of Thunder" or "Thunderbolts", which I guess was because they were fiery characters.

Street community is often *real* community, with unrelated people describing each other as "sister", "Nan", "Dad". Like any close-knit family, they will love each other, fight *for* and *with* each other, hug, fall out, and make up.

People without a physical home, often without any known blood relatives (because they've been bereaved, disowned or just lost contact), and often without a spiritual home, tend to find a sense of *belonging* in the street community that conventional society has denied them.

Here, there is no pressure to conform.

A place to be yourself – or whoever you want to be.

Herein lies one of the freedoms of the street.

So, coming back to "Doc" – we knew nothing about him, except that he seemed to know his way around Eureka, as he tried to lead us to a suitable place to sleep for the night, although we started to doubt this as he led us into a glass-strewn, deserted building, which even he seemed to decide was too unsafe..... and then led us out again.

Eventually the three of us settled, on Doc's advice, on a patch of pampas grass in the middle of some wasteland, where we soon got rained on.

Welcome to California.

Actually, California was good to us, with all kinds of unrepeatable adventures in Garberville, Humboldt County, where "California grass", as in *Get Back*, turned out to be all that we'd hoped and we hung out with another traveller called Jeff. Jeff was young, tanned and likeable, good-looking like Patrick Swayze, a dark horse with an elusive past. We camped by a river, where we fished and swam, ate wild fruit, stole food and Jack

69

Daniel's from local shops, ate in restaurants without paying, and lived wild in the country.

But, like most good times, the dream was to come to an end. As autumn approached, Helen toyed with the idea of returning to the UK to finish her degree at Dundee University. Despite my self-centred ways and fixation on Helen, I surprised myself by finding a genuine, selfless love inside me, that was willing to support her in whatever decision she made.

That very summer, Sting's *If You Love Somebody, Set Them Free*[25] had hit the airwaves and it seems the idea had lodged itself in my psyche. Was that God speaking to me through another '80s pop song? Maybe.

This was the one and only occasion, apart from flying, that we used public transport. Helen's Dad had wired her some money for a Greyhound bus from Garberville to San Francisco, then a plane home from there.

As I saw Helen off at the airport, courageously releasing her to follow her wishes, my heart was heavy. But we made a deal that I would continue the travels alone and see all the places we'd planned to see together.

It didn't take days, it took hours or minutes, for me to realise that I couldn't live without her. Not only was I a rootless young man with no sense of belonging other than with this girl, I'd been with Helen 24/7 for the last 6 months – an intensity of togetherness that not many adults experience. So it's not surprising the adjustment to being alone was somewhat *difficult*, leaving me feeling "bereaved and bereft", as Dire Straits sang that year in *Your Latest Trick*[26].

Somehow, the bottled-up emotion inside my bereaved and bereft heart energised me to walk mile after mile after furious mile – 20 or so in total –

---

[25] Sting, *If You Love Somebody, Set Them Free*, A&M, 1985.
[26] Dire Straits, *Your Latest Trick*, from the album *Brothers in Arms*, Vertigo, 1985.

along the fast freeways out of 'Frisco, back into the heart of rural California, after getting stoned halfway across the Golden Gate Bridge (a highlight, at the time, of visiting the city).

I had to be with Helen. Within days of parting, I was hitch-hiking the 2,500 miles across the breadth of the USA, from California to Newark Airport. It was the most incredible feat of hitch-hiking I ever achieved. Truck drivers would contact other truck drivers on their CB before dropping me off, to get me the next lift. I couldn't believe my luck. I made it across the States in 3 days, travelling day and night.

Unlike Supertramp, I didn't take the long way home...not that I had a home to go back to, either physically or spiritually. My homecoming was still a couple of years off.

During that 3-day trip I learned that a "bird dog" (a radar detector positioned on dashboards designed to give advance warning of speed guns) couldn't spot speed traps in sufficient time if the vehicle you're in is going over a certain speed. The truck driver I'd hitched a ride with was lucky just to receive an on-the-spot fine, one sultry New Mexico night on this racy trip, for going about 30mph over the 55mph speed limit, after being stopped on the I40 just outside Albuquerque. Unlike the 'M' for motorway in the UK, America has 'I' for Interstate – major freeways that dwarf our motorways and give a hint of the vastness of their country.

I also learned (not for the first time in my life) that the police aren't always great at searching vehicles for illicit substances, like the amphetamine pills stashed in a screwed up cigarette packet on the floor of the cab, of which we'd already partaken. At the time, I loved the irony of being stopped for speeding (as in the truck) but getting away with "speeding" (as in us).

And finally, I learned that you'll eventually crash (people, I mean, not vehicles) after going that long with virtually no sleep. Having paid for my flight back with the credit card that I'd kept for emergencies only and hadn't used in the USA till now, I slept the whole journey back to Gatwick from Newark, and was pretty miffed to have missed out on the in-flight meals!

After the long, dismal coach ride from London to Dundee – everything was a bit dismal in England after the States – the longed-for happy reunion with Helen finally took place. But the "happy" reunion was something of an anti-climax. Although we were back together, it was clear from that first, cold October moment at Dundee Coach Station that something had changed on Helen's side.

Helen was lodging with a family in a village called Errol, midway between Perth and Dundee, while she continued her studies at Dundee University. I managed to rent a room in a shared farmhouse just down the road in the same village. I had a place to stay, but still no sense of belonging, with nothing to do, no job to be found, no one to meet except a girlfriend who was fast becoming distant, and nothing else to live for.

For the life of me, I can't explain why I decided to buy a Bible during that period, except that I had time on my hands and, having always repeated parrot-fashion the second-hand claims of others that it was full of contradictions, like a lot of people who have never read the Bible, and having made baseless statements about the hypocrisy and stupidity of religious people, I suddenly thought it would be a good idea to read this ancient collection of books for myself and make up my own mind.

Of course, the Bible *is* full of contradictions and that's one of the wonderful things about it. There was a time, a few years ago, when I'd defend the Bible and explain away its apparent discrepancies. There may still be times when I would try and clarify how Jesus' teachings supersede some of the Old Testament laws that were only ever designed for the people of Israel anyway and not necessarily for global application.

But I love the paradoxes, contradictions and cryptic messages of the Bible. These are some of the things that make it so believable, reflecting as it does the reality of a messy world and the gamut of human experience.

I don't really know why I thought of delving into the Bible at that time, bar putting it down to divine nudging. And perhaps something inside me had begun to recognise my emptiness and need for *something*. I'd had no real contact with Christians, even in America. No other events or encounters that would make me want to investigate religion. Clearly, though, there was a shift in my head, a move towards a more open mind.

I found the cheapest Bible possible – an old, secondhand, pocket-sized, King James Version of the Bible for 10p from a charity shop in Dundee. I wasn't going to spend more than that on a *Bible*! My plan was to read through the whole thing – New Testament first, followed by the Old. An ambitious aim for a non-religious person who's never been a great reader. After absorbing a few chapters of Matthew's Gospel, the first book of the New Testament, I put the Bible down and soon forgot all about the reading plan. Not that I found it boring. Quite the opposite. Never having engaged with these profound, ancient texts before (despite the inoculating dose of empty religion at school), I was blown away by the Sermon on the Mount in Matthew's Gospel.

I still am. My heroes nowadays include those icons of nonviolent resistance, Gandhi and Martin Luther King, who were inspired by the Sermon on the Mount, whether they followed "Christianity" or not. King did; the Mahatma was turned off by the discrepancy between the words of Jesus and the actions of Christians.

When I read Jesus' words about not worrying about tomorrow, not worrying about meeting basic needs like food and clothing, because your heavenly Father knows your needs, it struck a chord with this then atheist in a way that makes no sense. I just instinctively sensed he was *right*. Even more striking was his teaching about forgiving people who hurt and abuse us, and loving our enemies. About a year later, in the winter of '86/'87, I shared a squat in Lewes with a violent, middle-aged, middle-class itinerant called Odin (nickname, again – in this case self-styled), who had come across "born-again Christians". He had a problem with these people because apparently they had told him that we should love *every*body. But we can't even *like* everybody, contended Odin, so how can we possibly *love* everyone? I had had no experience of any "born-again Christians", so I had no idea what he was talking about.

And yet, in early '86, in the solitude of my farmhouse room in the tiny village of Errol, Scotland, when I read about this attitude of loving enemies and forgiving the hurt people who hurt us, my reaction was "Wow! If everyone did this, it would end the endless vicious cycle of war and solve at least half the world's problems!" To me, it was a new, radical, earth-shattering idea that rocked my soul to its very core.

Although it was to be about another 18 months until I came to embrace Christ and Christianity, this was a quiet milestone moment that started to shape my life from somewhere deep within. I don't think I've ever been so deeply affected by anything I've read as I was in that Scottish farmhouse in '86.

So profound was the impact of reading the Sermon on the Mount that, when Helen left me for someone else, my response to her new lover was one that surprised even me.

Helen had been getting lifts into Dundee with Stuart, a hard, hairy biker guy, a *real man*, who also lived in Errol and had all the things I didn't have: car, job, motorbike, machismo, and (as it transpired) handgun. How could I compete with that? I was a dead-end loser with nothing going: no aspirations or opportunities.

So, having tried and failed to get hold of Helen on the phone one evening and the following morning, concerned in equal measure for her welfare and fidelity, I barged into Stuart's house and, after being threatened with the gun, pushed past him up the stairs to his bedroom, where my worst fears were realised. There she was.

The next thing I knew, I was being grabbed by Stuart and his friend, being thrown down the stairs, then picked up again by the arms and legs, and thrown out of the house on to the unforgiving gravel of the driveway. Humiliated, destroyed, body and soul bruised, this was the second and last time I ever considered suicide. My world had come crashing down; I had nothing left. In 1986 the Space Shuttle *Challenger* disintegrated and self-destructed to the horror of a watching world – the same year the flight path of my life took a similar turn.

Initial thoughts of topping myself and/or putting a brick through the windscreen of Stuart's car eventually (after drowning my sorrows in the pub, which didn't help at all) gave way to the astonishing decision to write a *letter of apology* to the man who had nicked my girlfriend and destroyed my world – an apology for barging into his house uninvited! It turned out that I was far more forgiving than the driveway.

Love your enemies. Overcome evil with good. Forgive those who hurt you. Even now, some 30 years later, I can hardly believe I did that. I wonder what Stuart made of the note. Maybe he wrote me off as a weirdo – or a doormat to walk over. Or could it possibly be that it made him examine his own life?

Maybe a chain reaction of love and forgiveness was kick-started through my response. It seems unlikely, but we never know what kind of butterfly effect our actions might initiate. I never did see him again, so I guess I'll never know.

Christians sometimes make colossal claims about the Bible, about it being infallible or inerrant. Although I wouldn't quite put it as strongly as that myself, I do share the view, from the experiences of others as well as my own, that the words of the Bible are able to speak creative, re-creative power beyond mere words into human hearts.

And perhaps even more so, that the words of *Jesus* have that incredible potential to change a person from inside out. In Christian circles, both the Bible and Jesus are sometimes described as "the Word of God", which can get a little confusing, as not many of us would put the Bible on the same level as the one we believe to be the Son of God.

To me, seeing Jesus as "the Word of God" means acknowledging that, just as at the beginning of time, when the breath of God's words exploded the Universe into being, with its ever-expanding ripples through space – in the same way, when we receive Jesus' presence into our lives, we are inviting the utterances of God that carry power to bring new life, a new existence. To me, it also means that through Jesus we have access to hearing the "words" (deep, felt senses and sometimes actual *words*) of compassion and grace, wisdom and creativity that emanate from the heart of the

Father. This may or may not come from the Bible, which serves as a spiritual signpost towards the *actual* "Word of God", Jesus Christ.

Looking back at the 20-year-old atheist that was the former me, that's exactly what I believe started to happen in the hidden places of my heart in response to those words of Jesus in Matthew's Gospel.

Does God speak to atheists through dreams, or the Bible, or mediocre '80s pop songs? Are atheists able to hear God's words? In my case, I think God started to awaken my dead, deaf heart during this period, through the Sermon on the Mount and perhaps even songs like *If You Love Somebody* and *Easy Lover*.

Contrary to the lyrics of the latter song, though, I've never regretted a thing. Even if the song was in any way an advance warning about an addictive love that was to be lost and crushed, the "easy lover" could just as easily have been me as Helen – and it's been clear in the years that followed that the whole crashing episode, just like Bruce (Almighty)'s crash, was all part of a greater plan to bring me to a new life and an even greater love – the Father's love, which in turn led me to a dependable *human* love.

Janine and I have celebrated our 20th wedding anniversary, a marriage built on the foundations of our shared Christian faith, and I can honestly say that her love, which flows from the Father's heart, has been a source of immense affirmation, strength and healing for me.

I guess there may be many people reading this who would probably be more convinced about the idea of God speaking through the Bible than through Phil Collins or Sting. And certainly, that encounter with the Gospel of Matthew had a far more profound effect than any song has ever had on my life.

The result of reading the Sermon on the Mount wasn't limited to that surprising response to Stuart. It turned out those inspirational teachings were to play a significant part in transforming my mind and soul when I got back on the road the following year, in a way that I couldn't explain, except in retrospective reflection.

7: Born to run

> *And may I just make my position very clear on this – there is no*
> *such thing as a FUN RUN as, even if you are dressed as an*
> *elephant, you still have to RUN. 'Fun' and 'run' are two words*
> *which, when the wonderful laws of Miranda-Land come into play,*
> *will be illegal to put together.*
>
> Miranda Hart

Obviously, the Boss wrote *Born to Run*[27] for me, in my runaway American dream. To live on the move, on the run, seemed to be my destiny. Thank God, I got cured of my need to *run away,* as he (God, that is, not Springsteen) gave me a spiritual home, as you'll read about later on, but I've needed no cure from being born to *run*.

The one thing I achieved during my period of lonely unemployment in Scotland was to train for and run in the 1986 Dundee Marathon. It was the one thing I did to relieve the boredom of my empty existence. I say "train for", but the truth is I knew nothing about running.

All I knew was that I needed good running shoes, and proudly bought a pair of Nike Pegasus out of my meagre benefits (in the days when Nike was just a good quality sports brand, before sports brands became designer labels), with their new, innovative air-filled soles, which served me well.

How did I afford these thirty-quid shoes out of my benefits? Well, for a start, I had no social life, no regular access to cannabis or any other

---

[27] Bruce Springsteen, *Born to Run*, Columbia, 1975.

substances, and used as little heating and electric as possible. On top of this, I regularly shoplifted most of my food, somehow managing never to get caught during the 6 months I lived in Scotland. I even stole all my loo rolls (those big super-size rolls) from a shopping centre toilet. When I read Janet and Allan Ahlberg's classic children's book *Burglar Bill* to my kids – a story about a man who lived in a house where everything he owned was nicked – I sometimes recall with a bit of an internal smile that I was once a bit like that.

Even so, most of the time I only just about got by on what I think from memory was about £30 a week.

I'm fortunate only to have had this one period of my life on benefits. Being dependent on the welfare system seems to be an excruciatingly demeaning lifestyle, one that most of the homeless and other vulnerable people I now work with are forced to endure – illustrated with disheartening realism by the Ken Loach film *I, Daniel Blake* in 2016.

In today's Conservative climate of benefit reductions, sanctions and rising prices, I'm incredulous that anyone survives and gets by, with or without food banks and other support agencies.

During my 3 months of training for the Dundee Marathon, I had a 13-mile flattish route that I ran 4 times / week round the Tayside country roads skirting heather-laden hills, with the occasional longer run of 18 or 25 miles. No other variation or gradual build-up. No wonder I suffered shin splints and knee pains.

On the day of the Marathon, I was so wired with adrenaline, I felt like I was bounding on springs, completing the first half significantly quicker than I've ever run 13 miles before or since: about 1 hour 20 mins. I felt like I could run at that pace *forever*.

I couldn't.

I inevitably flagged after a massively fast first fifteen miles, and ended up walking parts of the second half, yet still finishing in a very respectable 3:07.

That's my only real boast when it comes to running. My other running anecdotes are a bit more... entertaining.

***

....like the time at Ardingly College in my mid-teens, when I had the amazing brainwave of running the 25-mile sponsored walk that 2 coach-loads of pupils and teachers were going to undertake along the South Downs Way from Amberley to Ditchling Beacon.

Off I ran ahead of the coach party I'd arrived at Amberley with. Mile after mile I headed along the downland path, keeping on expecting to catch up with the first coach-load of kids that had gone ahead of us.

But I never did.

Which turned out to be because I'd been given the wrong directions from the start and had been going *west* instead of *east*. A minor detail to get wrong...

My lone, off-road marathon run along the grassy beauty of the South Downs turned into a mix of jogging west, then east, and somewhat worried hitch-hiking along grimy roads to the destination at Ditchling Beacon.

Taking place around 1980, before the days of mobile phones, GPS or health & safety, the teachers seemed to be entirely unfazed by my disappearance and eventual reappearance. They seemed more concerned with whether I had actually covered the sponsored distance – something I could only estimate from my haphazard escapade.

Despite – or perhaps because of – this early marathon mishap, I know I was *born to run*!

***

...or like the time more recently when, searching desperately for a loo mid-run in unfamiliar territory, in Kewstoke, Somerset, while staying with family, I found a village hall unlocked, crept in like Goldilocks, and with huge relief sat down in their gents, only to hear someone leaving the building a couple of minutes later and locking the front door behind them. Sitting on a toilet, trapped in a village hall in the middle of nowhere, I felt like I'd walked into a sitcom in which I played the starring role.

Miranda Hart, please feel free to use this material – my royalty fees are modest.

After a bit of minor panicking and wondering whether to search around in the upstairs office for a phone, I found one of those push-bar emergency exits that self-lock on closing. The relief of getting out unnoticed, without calling an emergency service, was as much of a relief as getting in to use the loo in the first place.

Despite – or maybe because of – episodes like this, I know I was *born to run*!

***

After the Dundee Marathon I planned to carry on running, but perseverance wasn't part of my make-up, and I finally returned to running at the age of 40 to celebrate my midlife (non-)crisis. Maybe the running helped *avert* a midlife crisis.

Despite the 20-year break, I know I was *born to run*.

Nowadays, that means running along the streets, seafront and woodlands of Hastings, and competing in occasional half-marathons, 5k and 10k races, with my weary, half-century-old body and worn-out knees.

It also means running with a vision I have for my life. From my first faltering day of Christian faith in '87, the restless energy I had within me was re-directed miraculously into an endless drive to use what I have to care for others. But more on that later, as we're only up to April 1986 so far in my story of spiritual homelessness and homecoming....

***

As well as energy to "run" with a vision, there's this physical energy and urge to literally run...and when my knees and other bits of me are too old and worn to run, I'll no doubt return to my former loves of cycling and walking.

But for now, I *keep on running*. And for me, the Springsteen classic is THE ultimate running song. You can keep your *Eye of the Tiger, Don't Stop Me Now* and all your dance music. *Born to Run* remains one of *the* best classics to play through my sweaty ear-phones as I plough up and down the hills of Hastings, where I find time to reflect, to enjoy the views and to be thankful that I no longer need to run *from* anything or anyone.

Thank you, Bruce, for the song.

8: No place like a squat

Listening is a magnetic and strange thing, a creative force. The friends who listen to us are the ones we move toward. When we are listened to, it creates us, makes us unfold and expand.
Karl A. Menninger

The six months spent in Errol were cold in more ways than one – the winter of my discontent.

With no reason to remain in Scotland after the relationship with Helen imploded, I returned in May '86, subdued and depressed, to Sussex, my home county. My Mum put me up in her flat where she was now living after the divorce, in the pretty, affluent, cliquey, intellectually elitist, county town of Lewes. Sorry, Lewes friends, for the description – I speak from my own subjective, not necessarily accurate, experience.

Evenings and weekends were generally spent in the escapist realms of hash and magic mushrooms with so-called "friends".

The mushroom trips were almost invariably *bad* or *really bad* – almost certainly linked to the low emotional state I was in. If the trips were always bad, why did I carry on doing it, you may wonder. I wondered that myself. Such is the irrationality of human nature, especially of people who are disconnected, with little sense of identity or belonging.

Although I was around other people a lot, the reality was that I had very few, if any, real friends around then. My old school mates were still scattered around the world or, like me, absorbed in their own problems. I made new acquaintances in Lewes through parties and pubs, but really there was very little in common apart from cannabis and beer.

The aloneness continued. During one mushroom trip in my mother's flat, while she was out, I cried solidly for hours, convinced that something was seriously wrong. I begged my "friends" to call an ambulance, which they refused to do.

Afterwards, I realised it was almost certainly the trauma of events in Scotland being unleashed in those tears. I'd had no one to talk to about what had happened in Errol, no opportunity to pour out my heart, so it was hardly surprising to find this huge outpouring of grief triggered by the influence of a psychotropic drug.

It became clear that, not only was I severely lacking in real friends, but I couldn't even necessarily *trust* the people I was hanging around with. Some jewellery belonging to my Mum went missing during that mushroom trip: one or both of my companions had taken advantage of the situation and rifled through her things while I was incapacitated by sobbing.

A few months later, a friend I knew only for a relatively short time *did* listen, and as I look back on my memories, this brief encounter with Gerard stands out as another milestone moment.

We were sat out in the late summer sun by the stream in Southover Grange Gardens. Always known as "The Grange", it was where Priory and ex-Priory kids spent endless hours hanging out. Gerard listened with real empathy and concern, without interrupting or judging; he showed genuine care.

For the first time, I heard myself recounting the events with Helen and Stuart, giving voice to how I'd felt. The painful reality of that traumatic time hit me like an intake of cold, fresh air. Sometimes it can be hard to comprehend what we've been through until we hear ourselves talk about it. Being listened to by an empathic friend or professional validates our experience and affirms *us* as people – which can be of particular importance if the sufferer already has low self-worth. It's often the first step in coming to terms with a loss or trauma. It's no surprise that many find counselling of such significant benefit.

The relief at being heard, believed and affirmed was huge...even if only a first step forward in the healing of a broken heart. A small step towards a homecoming.

In fact, pastoral counsellor David Augsburger goes so far as to claim that "Being heard is so close to being loved that for the average person, they are almost indistinguishable."

As part of my work role now, some 30 years later, I teach some basic listening skills as part of an induction training programme. I'm not a professional counsellor, but when I speak of the importance of active listening, I often remember the power of that simple interaction with Gerard, the significance of which he probably never realised.

The team I lead are used to hearing me reiterate the therapeutic value of listening; they're used to hearing me emphasise how easily we underestimate its positive impact. The annual service user surveys we conduct bear this out in the feedback we receive; clients express their appreciation at being listened to, particularly in a world of specialised and under-funded services, in which opportunities to "just" talk about their *lives in general* and about their *life stories in particular* are few and far between – in a world in which their friends may have too many problems of their own to offer an effective listening ear. Our service offers those opportunities.

I know what that's like.

***

Those Lewes days were spent shifting planks of wood around in my new job, working in a nearby timber yard.

Doing physical work outdoors again, in contact with these natural materials, was good, but still monotonous. Sometimes I'd sneak the odd joint behind stacks of wood, just to break up the day.

Work was nothing but a means to an end – saving up to go back on the road. I had unfinished business in the USA, after my time there the previous year had been cut short by Helen's return to Uni and my subsequent decision to follow her. There was so much more to see in that vast nation, and my aim was still to live life free, as an itinerant, a "bum". The plan was still to spend several years exploring the States, followed by India, then who knows.

As Arthur Daley once said, "The world is your lobster."

For the same reason as the timber yard job – saving up for a return to the States – I bought and sold small quantities of hash, always selling people a bit short, making sure I had some puff for myself as well as earning some financial profit. As far as I was concerned, cheating, stealing and lying was still the only way to get by in life.

For part of the winter of '86/'87 I moved out of my Mum's flat to stay in a nearby squat. This was no ordinary squat; no inner-city hell-hole; this was a *Lewes* squat, in keeping with the quaint county town! A pretty but abandoned, detached cottage that Odin had broken into.

Odin was a stocky, formidable man who talked to trees, toted tarot cards and had taken to the road in search of *something*. Perhaps he'd had some kind of midlife crisis; certainly he had some "issues" and was prone to severe violence if pushed. Not that I ever had any problem with him – in fact, we got on quite well, which is probably why it seemed like a good idea to move out of the comfort of Mum's flat to a squat with no heating or lighting. What it did have, though, was a back-burner: one night when we had a wood fire raging in the fireplace, we suddenly realised we had deliciously hot water on tap. Slinking into a steaming bath after this discovery was sheer delight.

Everything was a bit weird during that period. A trippy time in a purple haze of dope and mushrooms, infused with the sounds of The Doors, Hendrix, and *Sergeant Pepper*[28], with lots of people and a new girlfriend, but no real friends. A dark time, really, as 1987 dawned on the squat. And yet...

And yet...on the night of that New Year's Eve, something inside me told me that this was going to be a positive year, that something good was ahead. I just knew.

I guess that kind of feeling can either be some sort of prophetic instinct, or mere wishful thinking.

In my case, this portentous premonition couldn't have turned out any more different than I could ever have predicted, nor more accurate...

---

[28] The Beatles, *Sgt. Pepper's Lonely Hearts Club Band* (album), Parlophone, 1967.

9: Like a drifter

All shall be well, and all shall be well, and all manner of thing shall be well.

Julian of Norwich

What catches my memory's attention from my first steps back on the road in 1987 is not just events, but also thoughts and feelings, the most striking of which seemed to come out of nowhere.

As I stood by the side of the freeway, slightly daunted by the prospect of resuming the life of a hitch-hiker, I felt nevertheless inexplicably *positive*. On that very first day back on the road, I got chatting with another hitch-hiker. I told him about this "positive attitude".

Whatever had dawned on me on that New Year's Eve had stayed with me. I just believed everything would be *OK*: that I wouldn't really go hungry; and if I got attacked, I'd probably come out unscathed; but that if I *did* get attacked and even killed, somehow that would be OK too, because death wouldn't be the end.

The other hitch-hiker seemed to understand what I meant as, nodding in agreement, he told me about his own positive outlook on life on the road. I couldn't explain this. I *didn't choose* to have a positive attitude – I just felt this genuine confidence about whatever was ahead. I still had no belief in God – or *any*thing, although I knew by now that I was searching for *some*thing.

It was years later that I made the connection between that brief encounter with Matthew's Gospel in Scotland the previous year and this new, positive outlook. The Bible claims that its words have the power to catalyse faith. In years to come, it occurred to me that a seed of faith, sown through Jesus' advice about not worrying, was now germinating in the fertile soil of my unknown future on a wide open road.

It's not my style to Bible-bash – but the following short passage, which has influenced my life more profoundly than probably any other writing or saying by anyone ever (ever, ever...), warrants being quoted in full:

> "That is why I tell you not to worry about everyday life – whether you have enough food and drink, or enough clothes to wear. Isn't life more than food, and your body more than clothing? Look at the birds. They don't plant or harvest or store food in barns, for your heavenly Father feeds them. And aren't you far more valuable to him than they are? Can all your worries add a single moment to your life?
>
> "And why worry about your clothing? Look at the lilies of the field and how they grow. They don't work or make their clothing, yet Solomon in all his glory was not dressed as beautifully as they are. And if God cares so wonderfully for wildflowers that are here today and thrown into the fire tomorrow, he will certainly care for you. Why do you have so little faith?
>
> "So don't worry about these things, saying, 'What will we eat? What will we drink? What will we wear?' These things dominate the thoughts of unbelievers, but your heavenly Father already knows all your needs. Seek the Kingdom of God above all else, and live righteously, and he will give you everything you need."[29]

---

[29] Matthew's Gospel, chapter 6.

Looking back, those words were evidently instrumental in kickstarting this confidence in the future and, ultimately, even faith in God.

Somehow, the plan to save enough cash to return to the States, through a combination of working in the timber yard and selling cannabis, had come together, and by May '87, a year and a half after leaving the States the first time, I was back on the road.

After the previous experience of entering the States I was seriously sceptical about being let in – especially if Immigration had any record of my previous 5½-month overstay. They probably hadn't cottoned on to it, but I wasn't convinced.

This time, I was well prepared. I'd bought a return flight from the UK to Toronto with no intention of taking the flight back, and approached the States via Canada at the Windsor / Detroit border, all prepared to give some story about where I'd be staying once in the USA.

That way, if I was refused entry, I could always bum around Canada instead. Sweat literally poured off me as I passed through Immigration, fully expecting to be interrogated and disbelieved. To my amazement, I sailed through without question.

I'd put so much mental and emotional energy into the anticipated contest with Immigration that, once in, it occurred to me that I had no plan of where to go next!

Step 1 was complete; there was no Step 2.

Feeling at a loss as to what to do next, I spent a small chunk of the few hundred quid I'd come with on an internal flight from Detroit to Los Angeles, to visit my friend Nancy, who'd moved the previous year from the UK to live with her extended family in East LA.

So after a brief stay with this beautiful family (more on them later), it was on the roads out of LA that I was to embark on my second US hitch-hiking trip and experience those first glimmers of faith unexpectedly springing up within the recesses of my atheist heart.

On the very first day hitch-hiking, I recalled the Whitesnake song, *Here I Go Again*[30].

Here I was again, like a drifter, on the roads out of LA, slightly daunted, when I chatted with the other hitch-hiker about positive outlooks.

Here I go again, this time on my own, returning to the roads I knew, first of all to Garberville in northern California, then up into Oregon. Familiar places with fond memories seemed like a good place to start.

Although I started out by revisiting some old haunts from Trip No.1, those roads and places weren't the same on my own. Garberville felt empty without the previous company, Helen and Jeff, that had made the place as wild and free and hedonistic as it was. And I didn't stay.

In fact, the whole experience of life on the road in '87 turned out to be a far cry from '85. Not worse, in fact better, but very different.

While Trip No.1 had been a wild, romantic adventure, I relished the solitude and the freedom on Trip No.2 to do exactly what I wanted *when* I wanted, without having to refer to *any*one. I genuinely didn't miss the romance or the company, despite the empty experience of revisiting Garberville. The potential for impulsive moves from one part of the vast nation to another suited me to a T.

This was the total freedom from responsibility I'd always dreamed of.

---

[30] Whitesnake, *Here I Go Again*, Geffen, 1982.

Before leaving the UK, I'd brazenly burnt all boats to carve out that freedom – cleared out all my possessions except my rucksack, filled with what I needed for travelling; sold some of the record collection, gave the rest away; a friend gladly took my precious record player off my hands; I closed my bank account, but held on to the credit card as a back-up for emergencies only; resigned from my job at the timber yard; and callously dumped the girlfriend. Such was the self-obsessed drive to escape again, that even relationships were expendable.

Despite the important place music has always held in my life, my raison d'etre was not so much sex, drugs & rock 'n' roll as "sex, drugs & travel". There was no eternity in my heart, no purpose for life; the only thing worth pursuing, therefore, was hedonistic experience. Seeing the world, stoned.

The second stark contrast between the trips was the difference in attitude displayed by some people this time round, compared with when Helen had been with me. The absence of a pretty face beside me seemed to cause doors to shut in my less pretty face.

People who'd put the two of us up in '85 seemed to have lost all sense of hospitality – like Ed, the older guy who'd let me and Helen stay and given us some painting work, and Charlie the painter/decorator, who'd also given us work in '85, and whose doorbell I rang in vain in October '87 as I trudged through Denver in the falling snow.

Both men gave me a frosty reception. When Ed shut the door in my face on a late afternoon in Seaside, Oregon, a rage burned inside, that energised me to walk the furthest I've ever walked without stopping. Mile after mile I strode with furious vigour into the night, defiantly distancing myself from this cold seaside town, without a break, until after some 30 miles, at about 4am, I lay down by the side of the road to get some kip. Somewhere in the echoes of my mind I vaguely remembered something else I'd read in that short section of Matthew's Gospel about shaking the dust off your feet when people refuse you hospitality. I felt like I was doing just that in protest against the town that had rejected this traveller. Reflecting on the episode now through my middle-aged eyes, I tend to think: well, I was just a freeloading hitch-hiker; how dare my younger teenage self presume a right to hospitality from someone who hardly knew me, without so much as a phone call in advance?

I have no hard-and-fast moral conclusions, in relation to either Ed's *lack of* or my *presumption of* hospitality. What I see instead, in this event, are the stirrings of a passion in my own soul for hospitality and care for the homeless and transient.

Although faith in God hadn't yet emerged, embryonic values wrapped up in that yet-to-emerge faith were developing in the hidden places of my heart. Homes are for sharing; travellers and people without homes are people to be valued and assisted.

Hitch-hiking alone is no doubt a lot less dangerous for a single male than for a single female. Nevertheless, I did attract a fair share of sexual attention from gay men, including some who were only interested in giving me a lift in exchange for sex. When I turned them down, they drove off. Encounters like this coloured my thinking and caused me to become homophobic for many years. I thought: This is what gay men are like, only interested in one thing. It took me a long time to realise: This is what a lot of *men* are like, whether gay or straight.

In more recent years I've learned of the extreme dangers and abuse homeless women encounter at the hands of men. Very few women are found rough sleeping. One of the reasons for this is that homeless women often find men that will put them up in return for sexual "favours", rather than risk the (probably worse) dangers of sleeping on the streets; the knock-on effect of which is that they don't come to the attention of outreach workers and support services to the same extent, and are more likely to get caught up in a toxic trap of abuse and chronic homelessness. A May 2016 article in the Huffington Post, reporting on a research study with homeless women, explains this well.[31]

One homeless woman I've supported told me that she does occasionally find men who will let her stay at their place without expectation of anything in return, but these men are *rare*.

Sometimes I feel ashamed to be a man.

Men are to a greater or lesser extent driven by physical sexuality; at its worst extreme, expressed as complete objectification and abuse of women or other men. I eventually realised that what I experienced on the roads of America from a few gay men is what many women experience day in day out from straight men.

These experiences generally weren't traumatic, though, and one incident always stood out as funny.

There I am, sleeping on the sofa of a guy called Richard, when his gay brother walks into the house, off his head on alcohol and cocaine, and on seeing me on the sofa, stumbles into the kitchen to grab a weapon.

---

[31] Sophie Tanner. Homeless Women: If a Woman's Place Is In the Home... *Huffington Post*. 5th May 2016. http://www.huffingtonpost.co.uk/sophie-tanner/homelessness-women_b_9845804.html

He staggers up to me and holds the weapon to my neck, threatening to kill me if I don't take my trousers off. I turn to look, expecting to see a bread knife or something equally sharp, but instead I see a blunt fork... I suppose he could have done a bit of damage with it, but he was too out of it to exert any force, and the fork just seemed a joke in contrast with the anticipated bread knife. Richard came along, apologising for his brother, reprimanded him and sent him off to bed – which the guy sheepishly did!

I was left unfazed, and quite amused.

My homophobia was eventually dissolved by the twists and turns of later life and faith. Contrary to at least the public perception of Christianity, my faith compels a passion in me for the most marginalised, especially those who have been excluded historically by the church, and I've found myself blogging regularly in support of same-sex marriage and promoting a better understanding of sexuality among other Christians.

Jesus exhibited a burning passion for the "outsider": those on the edges of society, marginalised by socio-economic systems, or left "outside" of religious systems. The starkest demonstration of this is the infamous account of when Jesus, seeing the money-changers and sellers of sacrificial doves occupying the outer courts of the Jewish temple in Jerusalem, got REALLY mad! He made a whip, started chasing them out and literally "turned the tables" on them. Hence the expression.

The outer courts were the one space in the temple that was meant for the outsiders, people otherwise excluded by the religious system, to come and seek and worship God. Seeing their way to worship God being blocked by those who should have been including them prompted Jesus to display this "holy anger".

That's how strongly he felt about inclusion and making a way for ordinary people to find God.

The more I "see" Jesus, the more I long to see barriers that have been (often unintentionally) erected by churches, communities and systems come crashing down, to make a welcome for those they've excluded, whether LGBT, homeless or other minorities. This seems to me to be the heart of Jesus for churches, communities and...people.

There was at least one other important lesson I learned about prejudice and stereotypes during this trip. I'd recently ridden a freight train from Boise, Idaho, to Chicago, to spend some time with my sister, who was over in the States on holiday, following which the two of us hitched from Chicago to Detroit.

Before I continue this tale, did you see what I did there? A little, subtle boast of another form of hitch-hiking... Jumping a freight train was a delicious thrill, so different from any other form of travelling I've done. I crouched under a truck (lorry) trailer on top of a flat-bed train truck, for an epic 36 hours, lapping up the sweeping, changing scenery of the 1700 miles between the two cities, and getting utterly filthy from this open, grimy, thoroughly uncomfortable way of travelling.

I think the train climbed up over some mountains during the night, because it slowed right down for ages into the night-time hours and I froze to death.

Another traveller I'd met in Boise introduced me to the idea. Although relatively young, he seemed to be a seasoned hobo, who knew exactly where the trains were heading. He accompanied me for the first part of the journey to wherever he was going, then left me to continue on to Chicago.

When you ride a freight train, there are no station announcements, no guards, ticket collectors or other passengers to ask questions of. So finding I'd arrived at the right city after the journey halfway across the States was sweet joy, and for about a day and a half I'd felt like a real hobo.

It was fun and free, like so much about travelling America. That country may have mixed reputations, but for me in '87, it truly was the Land of the Free.

So I met up with my sister in Chicago, and from there we hitch-hiked for a couple of days to the centre of Detroit, where I left Ruth to take her bus into Canada.

I knew I couldn't realistically hitch a ride anywhere until I was out of the city centre, at the start of the freeway. So I walked. And walked. Down straight, wide street after straight, wide street, through the blazing city heat, towards the open road. Around 8 miles.

I'd heard rumours of Detroit's "bad areas", but knew nothing about them or where they were.

As I breezed through those suburbs with a brisk step, conscious of how conspicuous I was, a lone stranger with a big red rucksack, people sitting on the steps to their houses or chatting in the street would wave and call "Hi" with warm, friendly smiles.

Clearly this wasn't one of those bad areas.

It took me a while to realise it had been a very long time since I'd seen a white face – that all these friendly faces had been black. This white hitch-hiker with his great big rucksack, sticking out like a sore thumb in an all black neighbourhood, had received a beautiful welcome as he passed through.

Just as I was making this comforting observation, a big flashy car pulled up alongside me. Opening the window, the white couple inside, clearly alarmed at my presence there, gave me an urgent warning:

"What are you doing here? This is a really dangerous area. Let's get you out of here!"

"Nah, this is a *lovely* area," I replied nonchalantly. "People are really friendly," although I accepted the lift anyway.

Perhaps it *was* a dangerous area. Maybe it became alive and treacherous at night... Or perhaps I was just lucky that all the no-good hoods, dealers and gang members were off shopping or something that particular afternoon and that no untoward fate had befallen me. But my overriding impression was that I'd just encountered prejudice and assumptions about people because they were a different colour.

I may have been wrong, of course – after all, I knew nothing about Detroit – but whether I was right or wrong about the prejudices of white people towards this black neighbourhood is immaterial. The point is that certain values were beginning to form in my heart – around inclusion and overcoming potential fear through personal encounters with real people.

As I emerged safely out of Detroit, somewhere in my distant memory I recalled some religious words along the lines of "Even though I walk through the valley of the shadow of death..."

Maybe I *had* experienced some kind of divine protection. Maybe not. Who knows?

Of greater import was the fact that I even vaguely thought of those words from Psalm 23, suggesting that, alongside values around prejudice, fear and inclusion, some emergent thoughts of God and providence were also forming within.

Both strands of thought formed part of the journey home. Not that I was consciously looking for one, but a spiritual home was looking for *me* – was my destiny.

It's true that I was consciously looking for *something*, and that something was "Truth", even though I didn't think it actually existed! But the pursuit of Truth (in addition to sex, drugs & travel) seemed worthwhile, if only for the thrill of the chase.

I wonder why "Truth" was my thing. Maybe because I'd lived for so long in a state of dishonesty and my soul craved something better, more satisfying? Or maybe the search for Truth sprang from my first-hand experience of the vanity of the middle-class rat race – or that of the capitalist dream, so widely propagated in the '80s – that quite evidently could never deliver any of its empty promises. Or perhaps it was simply the emptiness of my own life experience that caused my soul to hanker after spiritual fulfilment. Maybe all those things.

Nietzsche claimed that a philosopher's system of thought always arises from his autobiography. In *Love's Executioner*, eminent existential psychotherapist Irvin Yalom makes the case that this theory holds true for anyone who thinks about thought[32].

My life seems to bear this out, not only because of the values embedded in my heart through these early experiences on the road, but also in more recent years, as my faith has morphed out of the mould of the sometimes rigid, modern evangelicalism into a more malleable, more ancient, contemplative Christian spirituality that's more at home with the

---

[32] Irvin Yalom, *Love's Executioner* (London: Penguin, 1991).

uncertainties and mysteries of real life, no doubt arising in part from working with people with complex needs.

In fact, I've long held the view that a Christian's genuine inner theology and view of God are shaped at least as much by his/her personality and life experience as by an objective interpretation of the Bible or church teaching – if not more so; hence, so much divergence amongst people of ostensibly the same faith. And wise church leaders recognise and accept this diversity of thought amongst their congregation or denomination.

***

My next physical destination was Gulfport, Mississippi, a mere 1,000 miles away. Soon after leaving Detroit, I managed to catch a lift all the way to Florida with a bunch of middle-aged guys in a hired MPV, who'd taken off on the spur of the moment after work one Friday, to spend the weekend in Pensacola. One of the guys had a daughter in the air force base in this southern coast city, and they'd decided to pay her a surprise visit.

They shared the driving, and even let me take a turn, but I was a bit out of practice and when I swerved badly on a major freeway while trying to adjust the driver's seat for my long legs, they quickly changed their minds! Still, they were great company for 24 hours. They shared their beers with me all the way down to Pensacola – and their whisky in the one motel room that we all stayed in, where they taught me poker.

That one night in Pensacola was all I ever saw of Florida. For some reason, the Sunshine State never had much appeal (and still doesn't), although one traveller I met suggested that to see the USA properly, you'd need to spend a year in each state – and I did consider trying to spend maybe a month in each and every state, including Florida.

It wasn't too far to hitch from Pensacola to Gulfport. During the period between the two trips to the States, I'd kept in touch with Jeff, who'd written to me telling me he was now in prison in Gulfport, and I'd determined to go and visit him.

It turned out that "Jeff" wasn't his real name, and while Helen and I had been camping with him in Garberville, he'd been wanted by the police for killing a man. We didn't know this at the time, but Jeff's way of getting by on the road was to "fuck over", as it was usually termed (i.e. mug), drivers who gave him lifts. I think he unintentionally killed someone in the process.

No wonder some people were so wary of picking up hitch-hikers.

Still, it was good to see this old friend again who probably didn't get any other visitors and seemed pretty pleased to see me.

A couple of years later, post-conversion and a short way into my nurse training in Eastbourne, I sent Jeff a Bible, thinking it was probably the best thing he could have under the circumstances. I remember the manager in the small post office in the Meads area of the town asking me if there was anything valuable in the package, and I told him in my still-new Christian passion, "Yes, this could save my friend's life!" I think I meant in more ways than one.

With no plans from here on, I drifted and slept rough in the Mississippi heat around the golden white sands of Biloxi. Here I learnt how to eat oysters off the beach (they weren't that nice) and waded in the warm, shallow, sheltered, waters of the Gulf of Mexico.

It wasn't like the misery of sleeping rough on the cold, wet streets of England, as too many people do, but having little or no money wasn't that great, either. And having been drawn into the street community of Biloxi,

I was talked into spending any money I did have on alcohol, not to mention selling my watch for beer too.

One guy I met in Biloxi would shoplift cartons of 200 cigarettes, to sell to truck drivers. I didn't need much persuading to join in this escapade. Unfortunately for me, the first time I tried it, I got caught with 2 cartons under my shirt.

The shop manager called the police, but while he was waiting for the cops to arrive, I legged it. I kept running till I found some woods to hide in. That was the only time I got caught shoplifting in the States, and I managed to get away with it. If the police had caught up with me, they probably would have seen that I'd overstayed my visa and I may even have been deported. Things would have turned out very differently.

Moving on from Biloxi, New Orleans was a compulsory stopping point, while I was in that neck of the woods. Unfortunately, I was literally, completely penniless and therefore, as much as I enjoyed seeing this compelling, iconic town, it was frustrating not to be able to visit any of the bars or music joints, so I only spent one night there. I got a meal at a soup kitchen and slept out on one of the hottest nights I've ever experienced: too warm even to have my sleeping-bag around me.

＊

Having said that certain individuals treated me very differently from when I'd been with Helen, nevertheless I encountered incredible hospitality and kindness from many strangers. As I mentioned, the USA has mixed reputations – it struck me as having the most extremes of everything, the best and the worst – but my experience of their warmth and generosity (at least to British visitors!) left me with a huge fondness for the American people.

103

It wasn't just the people, though, whose warmth I felt. There seemed to be some "warm love" from above, that according to Van Morrison is "everpresent everywhere"[33]. And it was this emerging spirituality that was *the* most striking difference between '85 and '87.

On the trip with Helen, we were pretty self-sufficient. We managed to get enough work to get by and never ran out of cash.

In '87, in contrast, money became scarce. I saw myself as "road-wise" rather than street-wise, and lived for the open road. City life's never been my thing. But when times were tough, I stayed in the cities to donate plasma for $5-$10 a time (depending on the city), which they'd let you do up to twice a week. The clinic would take a pint of blood, centrifuge it to separate the plasma from the red cells, and infuse the red cells back into the donor's bloodstream.

I have no idea what the screening procedures were like back then, but all the street people used to do it for a quick buck, and I became one of them.

At one clinic, while I was there, they treated and dressed a really nasty, infected ulcer that had developed on my elbow from a simple graze I'd sustained while messing around with a football in a field with Joel and Mikey in Portland. I found that every little scratch I got – and you tend to get a lot when you're sleeping rough – became infected. The elbow wound was so bad, I still bear the scar quite visibly 3 decades later.

The same thing happened to two symmetric wounds on my back that originated as simple scratches from the split rings on my metal frame rucksack when I walked or hitched with my shirt off in the southern heat.

---

[33] Van Morrison, *Warm Love*, Warner Bros, 1973.

Two decades later, in a physical assessment class as part of my nurse prescribing course, a medical lecturer demonstrating an examination of my back was trying to guess the cause of my scars and surmised I'd had some kind of thoracic surgery. I took great delight in revealing the real, obscure cause was my distant history of hitch-hiking.

My nutrition – and therefore immunity – was no doubt pretty poor, not to mention hygiene. I was never a proud, image-conscious young man – well, except in my younger punkier days, with my all-black clothes and hair. Showers weren't necessarily a priority when travelling, although I would find rivers to wash in, and one time discovered I could sneak into a high-class golf club through the back door to use their showers. That was luxury!

Homeless people are generally prone to infections, even if their hygiene is good. Like the rest of the population, many are keen to keep themselves clean and tidy, while others tend to let themselves go if their lives and energy are consumed by chasing the next beer or bag of heroin, or their minds distracted by psychotic illness or depression.

Many also have health conditions like hepatitis that affect their immunity, which in turn may also be compromised by poor nutrition.

When I was travelling, my weight dropped to about a stone lighter than for most of my young adult life – giving me a BMI of 18 (in other words, quite underweight) – and about 2.5 stone lighter than my current (healthy) weight.

For all these reasons, homeless people have high rates of respiratory, skin and wound infections.

Incredible to think, looking back on the elbow episode, that I'm now running homeless clinics myself, treating wounds, infections and other health problems; that I'm prescribing antibiotics, dressings and nutritional supplements. Who'd have thought it when I attended that plasma clinic in '87? Certainly not me.

Homeless people tend to have great difficulty accessing healthcare – even in the UK, where they don't have to have an address to be registered with a GP – although not all surgery staff realise this, unfortunately. Systems are difficult to navigate; making doctors' appointments is difficult even for people with the most organised lives; and healthcare often isn't top of the agenda for people in chaotic, vulnerable circumstances.

Despite the eternal, infernal funding challenges in the voluntary sector, I find it incredibly satisfying, working for a charity outside the NHS, to be able to offer informal, friendly, drop-in clinics, making healthcare accessible at venues where homeless people congregate; not being restricted to 10-minute consultations.

Talking of nutrition, I learned to raid the skips just after McDonald's had closed at night, for free, freshly discarded burgers while they were still warm! That was such a treat.

"Dumpster diving" as it's known in the US, or "skipping" in the UK, has hit the media in recent years as high-profile cases have heightened public pressure to reduce food waste by supermarkets and to legalise the practice of taking discarded food from skips – to criminalise supermarkets, not the poor and homeless, for this mad situation. It's been encouraging to see more scope being given for charities to at least accept food that's going out-of-date.

The other draw to the cities on my travels was the free meals in soup kitchens and hostels, which tended to be pretty grim, to be honest.

In one hostel, lying on a mattress on the floor of a grimy, bare room shared with a male stranger who had wanted to have sex with me, I clung on to my rucksack in my half-sleep, not trusting anyone.

But in every soup kitchen and hostel, the soup and sandwiches were a welcome relief to an empty stomach. Most were run by Christian missions and I'm forever grateful to all of them.

Some of these mission halls insisted on visitors listening through a gospel talk before being given food. Not too sure of the ethics of that now. And I'm not sure how receptive those raucous crowds with ravenous stomachs could have been to the messages being preached.

However, little bits of what I heard made me think, and I ended up debating and arguing one-to-one with some of the preachers. By this time, I had an interest in Buddhism and didn't much like these Christians' dualistic ideas of heaven and hell, God and Satan, good and evil, but something was beginning to chip away at me.

They preached about sin. As an amoral atheist, the concept of sin meant nothing to me. As far as I was concerned, if there was no God, then morality was meaningless and "sin" a non-concept.

But I had no doubt that, *if there were a God*, then I was a sinner and needed saving. My understanding of sin, if there were such a thing, was simplistic. My stealing, lying and deceitfulness, my general sense of being a bad person, constituted my sinfulness – *if* God was real. It was self-evident that my lifestyle constituted one of sin before the Christian god. If I could be convinced of the existence of God, I'd need no convincing of my sin. But if I continued in my atheism, I could continue in the dubious freedom of my amorality.

Many people never get past this kind of definition of sin – the things we do wrong and the shame we feel, especially in the presence of religion. That same year the Pet Shop Boys released *It's a Sin*[34] that so mournfully depicts the "Catholic guilt" experienced by singer/ songwriter Neil Tennant and unfortunately so many others brought up with shame-drenched religion. To Tennant, everything about his life was "a sin". When I read how he claims to have written the lyrics in just 15 minutes in an outpouring of anger and frustration at his Catholic upbringing (which perhaps especially plagued his life as a gay man), my eyes filled with tears for him. I long to tell people like him, "You are good"!

After winning a dispute with Jonathan King over claims that they had plagiarised the melody for this song, the Pet Shop Boys donated the out-of-court damages to charity. How beautiful is that? Tennant has also gone on to be an advocate for LGBT issues and social justice. Tennant, you are good.

Henri Nouwen, the renowned Dutch Roman Catholic priest who, as pastor within the L'Arche Daybreak Community in Toronto, spent the latter years of his life with adults with learning disabilities, tells in *The Return of the Prodigal Son* of how he had been so warned against pride and conceit that he considered low self-esteem to be a virtue.

> "But now," he says, "I realize that the real sin is to deny God's first love for me, to ignore my original goodness. Because without claiming that first love and that original goodness for myself, I lose touch with my true self and embark on the destructive search

---

[34] Pet Shop Boys, *It's a Sin*, Parlophone, 1987.

among the wrong people and in the wrong places for what can only be found in the house of my Father."[35]

Brian Thorne, the celebrated spiritual (Christian) psychotherapist, takes the same line in his short, reflective book *Behold the Man* by observing that:

"It is the therapist's task...to bring such people to an awareness of their own identity and to a trust in their own essential value and goodness."[36]

I identify with Nouwen and Thorne in my work with vulnerable and broken people, as well as in making sense of my own life. Thorne's observation is one of the reasons I'm drawn towards training as a counsellor.

In view of its association with religious shame as portrayed so vividly by the Pet Shop Boys, it's not surprising that "sin" is an unpopular idea. This and the general confusion over what sin means are perhaps the main reasons why, as much as I recognise its reality, I tend to shy away from the word.

And no wonder confusion reigns when it comes to sin. The best theologians, even the Bible writers, have struggled to pin it down between various ideas of selfishness, missing a moral target, failing to love God, failing to treat others as we would want to be treated, or trespassing across moral boundaries. All of these are jigsaw pieces, perhaps, that form part of the picture of what theologians mean by sin.

---

[35] Henri J.M. Nouwen, *The Return of the Prodigal Son* (London: Darton, Longman & Todd, 1994).
[36] Brian Thorne, *Behold The Man* (London: Darton, Longman & Todd, 2006).

However, there's one other way of looking at the word that appeals to this person who's been drawn into the caring professions with a passion for whole-person healing, and I'm unashamedly biased towards this particular image of sin because it's one that Jesus emphasised.

It's the idea of sin as a *sickness*. When criticised for hanging out with "sinners" by the moral police – the Pharisees, who were bent on piling religious guilt on the common people, in the way that Tennant experienced at the hands of modern-day Pharisees – Jesus likened himself to a doctor spending time with people who needed help and healing. "Sin", according to Jesus, has connotations of illness – something that pervades our being, that's somewhat out of our control, for which we need outside help. It seems to imply aspects of both doing wrong and being wronged. I think this is one of the reasons why 12-step programmes work for many people, because they deal with the two faces of our brokenness – victim and perpetrator – which lie at the heart of our very human addictions.

Jesus' approach to sin carries the sweet aroma of compassion and empathy. People laden with guilt and addiction were drawn to his love, not repulsed by judgmental morality.

Sin in the presence of man-made religion inevitably breeds shame, while in the presence of Jesus and those who reflect him in this world it attracts compassion, understanding, and the possibility of freedom.

As the song goes:

> *Where the wrongs we have done*
> *and the wrongs done to us*
> *were nailed there with him,*
> *there at the cross.*[37]

In the hostels and homeless missions, I was starting to question my non-belief in God and sin, while at the same time experiencing occasional encounters with the judgmental side of Christianity. And yet, somehow, these weren't enough to put me off the scent of Jesus.

In one place, my rucksack had been searched, revealing my 6-inch camping knife. I explained truthfully to the hostel staff that I used it for everything from building fires to making sandwiches. I was never a violent person and, although I told them I would use the knife in self-defence if pushed, I probably would never have even done that. I received a lecture about carrying knives from this "preacher" who didn't believe my story that it really wasn't being carried as a weapon.

In another memorable instance of facing disbelief and distrust, I approached a Salvation Army mission to ask for a sleeping-bag, after mine had been stolen. Maybe they thought I wanted another to sell on. They gave me one eventually, only with great reluctance.

Despite this one untoward incident, I've retained a fond affinity with the Salvation Army, who helped me out on many occasions.

However, being judged, accused and having assumptions made about them is something homeless people in any country encounter constantly.

He's chosen to be homeless.
She's an alkie, a junkie.
It must be his fault he's ended up like that.
Why doesn't he get a job?

---

[37] Randy Butler & Terry Butler, *At the Cross*, Mercy/Vineyard Publishing, 1993.

In my role with homeless people today, I remember what it's like to be judged and disbelieved. I remember that there's usually a complex story behind a person's homelessness. Even though I wasn't forced out on to the streets like many others, there *were* complex reasons behind my own choice to live homeless and it's my hope that the individuality of my story will help to illustrate the uniqueness of every homeless person's journey. I try and keep an open mind when clients talk of their woeful circumstances and traumatic pasts. Sure, people don't always tell the truth and I might be a soft touch at times, but I endeavour to avoid jumping to conclusions either way and would far rather err on the side of trust and give that person the dignity of being believed.

As Jean Vanier so eloquently put it,

> "To love someone is not first of all to do things for them, but to reveal to them their beauty and value, to say to them through your attitude, 'You are beautiful. You are important. I trust you. You can trust yourself.'"[38]

When we judge and distrust vulnerable people, we denigrate them, we diminish their already low self-worth and the capacity to climb out of their pits. They become even further disempowered.

I heard a lovely, young, ex-homeless lady at a conference speak about how, at the age of 15, a doctor had laughed after she asked him what he meant by his question, "Do you hear voices?" Whatever the reason for his laughter (perhaps he was nervous, or surprised at her request for clarification), she was unable to talk about the voices in her head for

---

[38] Jean Vanier, *The Broken Body* (London: Darton, Longman & Todd, 1988).

many years after feeling she'd been mocked or taken less than seriously by this health professional.

That one inappropriate response from someone in authority contributed to that girl being imprisoned by her mental health disorder for too many years. A gentle, empathic approach might have helped to unlock her chains.

In a similar vein, I love to engage in debate about begging. I like to start with the pros and cons of giving money: "do you / don't you?" I don't necessarily advocate giving money to people for drink and drugs, which we know is the reason for most people begging, in the UK at least – but they're going to obtain the money they need one way or another, so it might as well come from someone like you or me giving willingly out of a generous heart rather than by shoplifting or something worse. That's one way of looking at it.

More important than that question, though, is the attitude we display. I like to encourage people to realise that when they see someone begging, that person has reached a real low point to be in that position. The self-worth of that "poor beggar" is probably at rock bottom. They're most likely depressed, and maybe in the grip of a life-destroying addiction. They may well be homeless. Not everyone begging is homeless, and not all are at rock-bottom (some are simply "addicted to the streets" and revel in the social interaction with their regular donors) but many are.

To engage in conversation, to give them the time of day or at least a smile, is perhaps the most valuable thing we can do. To promote their sense of being a precious human. If we have time and confidence to find out a bit about their lives, maybe even build a rapport, even better.

Similarly, Dr Viktor Frankl, reflecting on his experiences in a Second World War concentration camp, describes an occasion when a guard secretly gave him a small piece of bread saved from his own ration. Frankl says that what moved him to tears was far more than that small bit of food:

> "It was the human 'something' which this man also gave to me – the word and look which accompanied the gift."[39]

Trust, love and dignity go a long way towards empowering vulnerable people to make positive changes.

If we can achieve some of those things, then whatever we give, or whether we give at all, becomes almost immaterial.

I feel incredulous when I hear (less often these days) of people buying a Big Mac or a coffee for someone on the street without asking the person first. Even destitute people have likes, dislikes, and the need to make choices. However kind it may seem, these unsolicited actions probably do more to assuage the giver's sense of guilt or duty than to build the dignity and self-worth of the recipient, demonstrating more pity than compassion.

***

Although my experiences of living on the roads and streets of America were very mixed, every aspect was part and parcel of a spiritual journey, and despite the instances of being (mis)judged and the times of destitution, I never worried.

Through it all ran a golden thread of unexpected allurement towards faith in God – a double-stranded cord of experiences and conversations that

---

[39] Viktor Frankl, *Man's Search for Meaning* (London: Rider, 2004), 94.

awakened my previously unspiritual heart to the possibility and providence of God.

Each time the kindness of a stranger was shown to me at *just the right time* – being given money just when I'd run out, being offered a place to stay *just when I needed it most* – I started to say, "Someone up there likes me!"

It was a joke to begin with.

The timeliness astounded me – in fact *spooked* me – to the point where I began to say, with just a little bit of genuine awe, almost fear: "Maybe someone up there *really does* like me!"

Such serendipity seemed to suggest that, in the words of Steve Winwood, "there must be Higher Love"[40] behind the kindness and warmth of these strangers.

One example of this serendipity happened when I spent those couple of days hitch-hiking with my sister from Chicago to Detroit. Between leaving the freight train and meeting Ruth in Chicago, I'd lost a $20 bill, leaving me with $8 to my name, with no prospect of any money coming in from anywhere. No work or benefits.

We caught a ride with a father and son who were on their way to a Pentecostal conference in Detroit. Ruth and I sat in the back, as the middle-aged son drove, with his elderly Dad in the front passenger seat. During the journey the old man turned round, and without so much as a word to ask our consent, took hold of our hands and prayed the longest, fervent, heartfelt prayer for us. I've never remembered what he prayed,

---

[40] Steve Winwood, *Higher Love*, Island, 1986.

but I've never forgotten the effect: I felt uplifted, upbeat, like nothing could go wrong.

This Christian father and son, as they dropped us off in Detroit, not knowing about my $20 loss, gave me and Ruth a $20 bill each. Ruth left the whole $40 with me, as I had the greater need. It seemed like God or *Something* had doubly covered my loss.

Coupled with this, the prayer left me fearless as I strode through those streets of Detroit. And there seemed to be a link between the two.

Another time, after spending the night in a homeless hostel in Kansas, I stepped out onto the simmering early morning city streets with no money, no food, and one cigarette to my name. I'd just walked out the door when I was approached by a stranger asking for a cigarette. "Why not!" I thought, and gave him my last smoke. I basically had nothing now. Later that day, a driver I'd hitched a lift with offered me a cigarette, which I accepted. As we continued along the freeway, he told me that he'd gone to buy his usual pack of cigarettes that morning, to find that they were buy-one-get-one-free this particular day, so he gave me one of the packs, not knowing about my gift to a stranger that morning.

I have never believed in karma. Not then. Not now. Since then, I've come to believe that there is a God who is far better, more forgiving, than the merciless eye-for-eye-dea (see what I did there) of karma and much religion, but it did seem at the time that Something-that-could-be-God had given me 20 times return on my giving.

Maybe I should mention that I'm not advocating smoking. In fact, I quit cigarettes just a few months later, and now provide stop smoking support and prescribing in my work. But smoking's not a crime or even a "sin", really – except perhaps against ourselves, and even then, in "moral" terms no worse than eating too much saturated fat or over-working – and it does seem in hindsight that God used many "coincidences" like this to open my mind and heart to him.

Mere coincidence? (These were two of many.) Could be.

Leading psychiatrists in Carl Jung's day criticised him for his quasi-spiritual concept of *synchronicity* – a word he coined to express the idea that *coincidences have meaning.*

Nowadays I have no hesitation in ascribing divine purpose to fortuitous coincidences, and of course I'm no means alone in that. Probably a large percentage of the world's population, and even a foremost psychologist such as Jung, would say in the face of a serendipitous meeting or finding that something was "meant to be", that "God had willed it", or "it was fate".

It's of curious importance to me that from the very start of existentialism, two branches of the school of thought emerged: one driven by the atheism of Nietzsche, Sartre and others, which assumed that there was *no obvious meaning* to existence; while in contrast the other branch, influenced by the likes of theologian Kierkegaard, assumed that each person has an innate *need for* meaning. The latter branch made no definite assumptions about whether or not that meaning was there to be discovered.

My overwhelming sense, from numerous occasions like these, was of being protected and provided for by something that *could be* God. I'd agree with the existentialists that that feeling of divine providence behind happy events originated, in part at least, from a need for meaning in my life.

The question that many would seek to answer is whether my growing interpretation of events was *true* – whether the meaning I was beginning to attribute to my experiences was genuine or simply wishful thinking. I guess that question can never be conclusively answered either way, just as "proving" the existence of God is a fruitless task.

My best answer, however, is this: that the strongest evidence for the reality of divine provision and calling towards God in this whole trip around the States is the deep and lasting change in my life from the inside outwards, from my first steps into faith a short time later and over the next 3 decades, right up to today – as presented over the following chapters.

Also, Christianity or theism was definitely *not* what I was looking for. It was like *it* (or God) chose *me* rather than the other way round. "You did not choose me, but I chose you," as Jesus once said to his followers.

For now, though, I was nowhere near ready *yet* to say that I believed, but I couldn't help but wonder.

***

Concurrent with these experiences were conversations with people who gave me lifts and told me about how their lives had been changed since putting their faith in Jesus. Over time, my arguments gradually gave way to questions.

This was especially true of my dialogue with painter/decorator Ray Galloway, who gave me work over two periods of some weeks in Portland, Oregon. Sarah Edelman had put me in touch with him when I'd been looking for work.

Ray had been a Christian for only about 3 years and told me of what Jesus had done in his life. I can't even remember now what these changes were

– what impressed me more was the way he worked with honesty, integrity, and professionalism, always doing *extra* rather than less.

As a result, he was recommended by one customer to the next. He didn't need to advertise, and business was booming. This was such a contrast to the only way I knew to get by in life: cheating, stealing, lying and freeloading. This honesty stuff actually *worked*!

The same principle is now an integral part of my personal values, first witnessed in and modelled by Ray, now infused by my own faith. God's Spirit energises in me a drive towards integrity, honesty and generosity. And that seems to work on many levels, just like it did for Ray, even if I don't always get it right.

In my own particular context, genuineness, honesty and trust are essential ingredients of the therapeutic relationship, particularly when working with vulnerable people whose lives have been marred by broken trust and abuse. They need to be able to see that the staff and volunteers (and, ideally, friends) supporting them are genuine and trustworthy. That therapeutic relationship, even with paid professionals, has been found in numerous studies to be a source of immense healing.

I've consistently seen how homeless people will inevitably gravitate towards workers they trust and relate to – who they know will be there for them and keep their word. Within such relationships, even the most traumatised individuals can start to believe in the possibility of change and healing. Similarly, the purpose of therapists, according to Jan Hawkins "is not to make people feel better, but to *provide the circumstances* in which the person can contact their inner resources to grow"[41] (italics mine).

What also struck me about the Christians I met on the roads of America was the way their faces (including Ray's) seemed to shine with the light, or joy, they claimed to have found in Christ. They say the eyes are the window to the soul, and it was like whatever was in these people's souls couldn't be hidden. It leaked out, through their eyes.

There was something very real and alive about their faith – which I didn't see in the faces of other faiths I met along the way, like the many Mormons and the occasional Jehovah's Witness or Buddhist, who seemed to be simply promoting a belief system rather than demonstrating a changed heart that had been brought to life by an unstoppable power with authentic passion.

This series of encounters stood in stark contrast with the trip of '85. Strange how Helen and I never encountered religious people, Christians or otherwise, trying to convince us about their faith, yet now in '87 when my heart had been humbled by events in Errol and my soul had begun to search for "Truth", it seemed to be Christian after Christian who gave me lifts and spoke to me about their lives.

Personally, I'm certain that our times are in God's hands.

It's not uncommon to hear people (of any or no faith) who work with homeless people and addicts speak of right timing. In the world of vulnerable people and addiction, the Universal principle of timing speaks loudly. Individuals entrenched in addiction and/or homelessness seem only to be able to make changes when the time is "right" for them: a moment that seems to be nigh-on impossible to predict.

---

[41] Jan Hawkins, in a chapter entitled: Walking the Talk: Potent therapy is a risky business. In Jeff Leonardi (ed.), *The human being fully alive* (Ross-on-Wye: PCCS, 2010), 26

Serendipitous circumstances, a "rock bottom" experience, an encounter with grace, or simply the person coming to a place of readiness to change for no obvious reason...there just seems to be a right time for everyone. Does that mean we sit back and wait till individuals are ready to change? Absolutely not. Knowing that people who care (or even just *someone* who cares) – who have been waiting in the wings till the time is ripe, may play a crucial part in the recovery of an addict or an entrenched rough sleeper. We keep expressing our concern, our offers of support, even if those offers are spurned, until that person demonstrates readiness to engage with help and potential to change. Then *bam!* – recovery is possible.

At this very moment, I'm about to take a break from writing this in order to ring a friend about the possibility of his entering rehab. Michael is caught up in a tangle of drugs, crime (in which he is both perpetrator and victim), poverty, deceit, deteriorating health, confusion, and the unnecessary shame of having dropped out of church.

I say "unnecessary" because I know without a shadow of a doubt that everyone at church would welcome him back with open arms and not an inch of judgment. Shame is a common, antagonising, key player in the vicious circle of addiction, often multiplied several-fold for someone with faith who has known better times. All the words of grace and kindness and forgiveness from well-meaning Christian friends like me seem to fall on deaf ears when it comes to someone like Michael, entangled in that web of shame.

Whether Michael is ready for rehab, I don't know. I'm prepared for it to work out or not. Either way, I and other friends will be there for him, no matter what, until the time is right.

***

There's another reason for those hitch-hiking conversations of faith to have taken place in '87, and not in '85 with Helen: people are usually far more ready to discuss matters of faith and spirituality and meaning on a one-to-one basis. Sharing those deepest thoughts and questions that we have about life can be an intensely personal, even vulnerable, experience. As my dormant eyes began to open to the possibility of an Unseen Hand assisting me and my physical eyes saw travellers who carried nothing, I started to feel burdened by the big frame rucksack on my back with my sleeping-bag, tent and clothes, and wished for the opportunity to see whether "God", if he was there, would provide if I had literally nothing! Also, I was hardly spending more than one night in any one place, so I tended to sleep beneath the stars, rendering my heavy 2-man tent almost superfluous.

A strange wish, perhaps, but I've never felt tied to possessions and still longed for an even greater freedom.

***

If you're as old as me, you'll probably remember those *Top of the Pops* records from the 70s – the precursors to *Now That's What I Call Music*. The main difference being that, unlike *Now...*, the *TOTP* albums were dirt cheap records from Woolworth's that didn't feature the original artists but cover versions, or rather imitations, by session musicians. Hard to imagine anyone would buy those nowadays, although actually the recordings weren't *that* bad, in my opinion.

The first record my sister bought was a *TOTP* record in 1973, which included a cover of Roger Daltrey's beautiful *Giving it all Away* (written by Leo Sayer)[42].

Ruth, being older, was into music earlier than I was, but I equally enjoyed listening to her records on our family's ancient, wooden-cased radiogram. The sound of the vinyl discs plopping down the steel spindle on to the hard, rubber turntable, to produce those solid, scratchy tones was literally music to our young ears.

As I grew older, I'd sometimes recall those nostalgic sounding words from *Giving it all Away* that so resonated with me.

My aim from early years to be possession-less apparently sprang from unhappy childhood days, with which I associated materialism. In preparation for this second venture into America (and thence the world, although that was never to be), I'd given almost everything away. I just had the possessions on my back; now I craved freedom from these.

Later, looking back, I could say, a bit like Daltrey, that I was just an immature young man trying to make sense of his world, trying to find freedom, believing it lay in the absence of possessions and responsibilities, not discovering till much later that true freedom is not to be found in the absence of anything but in the *quality and type of relationships* that we have with things, with ourselves, with others and with God.

Or, in Tolstoy's words, which my life bore out:

> "We don't reach freedom searching for freedom, but in searching for truth. Freedom is not an end, but a consequence."

Even as I settled as a young Christian over the ensuing years into a semblance of "normality" as understood by sanitised society, it took me a long time to give up giving everything up. Although giving everything away

---

[42] Roger Daltrey, *Giving It All Away*, Track, 1973.

may sound like a noble habit – even a "Christian" thing to do – it belied some vestiges of my earlier dysfunctionality.

I had an unhealthy relationship with possessions and money – an infantile aversion to bearing the responsibility of ownership. In those first years of my new life, I continued to keep possessions to an absolute minimum and purposely lived well below my means as a young single student nurse and then staff nurse, preferring to support charities or friends with the rest rather than ever think about holding on to any money for saving or spending on myself – an attitude that had as much to do with low self-esteem as selfless generosity.

Now I'm less dysfunctional and value myself more highly. I hope I haven't lost too much of that spirit of generosity, though. I still retain a certain degree of (healthy) non-attachment to possessions and there remains a sub-surface wish to have less, but I've also learned to live with possessions, a house with a mortgage, the responsibility of ownership and all that jazz, and try to use my state of privilege for the benefit of others.

***

But back to the story, in 1987, when freedom from responsibility and possessions was the only kind of freedom I knew, and a secret longing was growing for liberation even from the belongings on my back.

One night, my wish came true.

I'd ended up travelling with Richard for a few days – Richard, with the brother of blunt fork fame. Like his brother, Richard was also gay and was moving to a new city with a rucksack full of precious clothes and bling – tons of gold jewellery and the like.

124

As two men hitch-hiking together, it can be pretty difficult to catch rides, and we found ourselves stuck on the side of the on-ramp (slip-road) to the freeway. Thumbs outstretched, going nowhere, as dusk fell.

What happened next was an incredibly stupid thing to do, but chaotic, messed-up people aren't known for making the smartest decisions. We hid our rucksacks in some bushes close to the freeway and walked to the nearby town where we'd heard there was a hostel. The next morning we returned to our rucksacks, to find a few of our possessions strewn around the ground and the rest gone! All Richard's gold jewellery. My passport, credit card, tent, sleeping-bag etc. All gone.

Understandably, Richard was furious. I didn't like to admit it to him, but I felt relieved at the prospect of travelling *ultra*-light and strangely happy with anticipation at a new opportunity!

However, losing my passport meant that I was a non-person in the USA. It certainly felt like that. Having no ID meant I could no longer donate plasma – my only meagre source of income. And loss of the credit card meant there was now no back-up plan.

We ended up in Denver, sleeping in a doorway in the pouring rain, with no sleeping bags, no nothing. It was a pretty wretched night. Thankfully I didn't have too many nights like that. It was soon after this when the Salvation Army mission hall in Denver reluctantly issued me with that sleeping-bag.

Before long, I resumed my preferred mode of travelling – i.e. alone – eager to see whether "God" would provide. Very soon, I was taken into the home of a wonderful couple, who gave me everything I needed for the time being.

Whether this was simply human provision, or a hand from above, or both, I had a growing sense of being "called" by God to put my faith in him. Through it all, I became increasingly awed by vast American landscapes, jaw-dropping sunsets, star-laden nights, and the universe in general. I became more and more perplexed by how and why anything existed. I'd read a bit about quantum physics on the road, and became intrigued by the unpredictable, chaotic nature of the subatomic realm – an unseen world that epitomised just how out-of-human-grasp-and-control the universe really Is.

As time and hitch-hiking miles went on, as my mind and heart meandered through musings of Buddhism, quantum physics and Christianity, I had a growing sense of getting closer to that elusive thing called "Truth" which I paradoxically never expected to find. And Christianity was not the destination I expected.

But my mind was shifting from thinking how ridiculous it was to believe in God and how religion was simply a crutch for the weak, to considering with growing conviction: "How could there possibly *not* be a God?"

The sheer incredibility of existence increasingly, for me, pointed towards a Maker, a Designer.

Even Whitesnake, in the aforementioned song, pray to God as they search for answers while walking the lonely road!

***

Now that I'm lucky enough to own a comfortable house with wide, glass patio doors, almost every day I enjoy watching the many sparrows and other birds take advantage of our seed and nut feeders.

Nearly every day the birds remind me of those words of Jesus: that God is faithful and will take care of our needs; that if he cares about the sparrows, then he will certainly look after us humans too.

And sometimes, watching the birds eat the food that *I've* put out, I remember that often God answers prayers for provision through other people, and that I need to be ready to be the answer to someone else's prayer, like Michael's, for practical help, support, friendship, maybe even finance.

Not that those "prayers" are necessarily faith-filled spoken words from religious people to God; "prayer" is very often an inner, silent cry from a desperate heart that has no belief in God, but which he nevertheless will always hear. As I mentioned, I believe that God believes in atheists.

And I remember that sometimes even I – Mr Independent – need to be humble, willing and able to accept the support of others as an answer to my own prayers and needs.

Although I'm aware that in many ways it was far easier not to worry when I was young, free and single, on the road with no responsibilities, when I observe the birds pecking away at the seeds I recall how my own experience bore out those assurances from Jesus; and my faith reminds me that, even though I now have a family and a mortgage and absurd food bills, *he* hasn't changed.

Thank you, sparrows, for reminding me that "all shall be well, and all shall be well, and all manner of thing shall be well."

10: Like a rolling stone

Loneliness and the feeling of being unwanted is the most terrible poverty.
Mother Teresa

I only ever took acid once, despite having taken magic mushrooms numerous times. Not for lack of wanting to – just that it only came my way the once.

After staying with truck driver Carl and his wife Sarah in Portland in '85, I'd kept in touch with Sarah, who was now unfortunately separated from her husband. Unlike Charlie and Ed, Sarah kindly resumed her hospitality for two periods of a few weeks in 1987 and introduced me to Ray Galloway.

Joel and Mikey, Carl and Sarah's teenage sons, took me under their wing and introduced me to their drug-fuelled partying lives. It was a lot of fun. One particular highlight was a GBH gig, which was amazing, seeing British punk played to an American audience! Much more fun and happy than the British gigs I was used to, where punks were so sombre and serious. One particular night in Sept '87, a lot of weed had been smoked, and a fair amount of crystal meth snorted, before we each took a single acid (LSD) tab. It seemed to take several hours for us to "come up" on the acid – then in the early hours Joel invited me for a drive down the freeway. He liked to night-drive while tripping.

Remember the racing car game, Pole Position? Maybe you're too young? As well as Pacman, I used to play this in the Brighton arcades instead of attending A-level classes, and now with all the lights and coloured cat's eyes, the road before us had become an animated arcade screen, like Pole Position. *Only even more vibrant.*

As we drove in spaced silence, I assumed that Joel was sharing the same experience.

Wings' *Band on the Run*[43] played in crystal clear, Dolby quality in my head, and I assumed this was running through Joel's head too, as he drove quietly and confidently down the empty, night-time Oregon highway.

Later, though, *Like a Rolling Stone*[44] came on the radio, for real, Dylan interrogating me with incisive questions about my itinerant life. *How does it feel...* to be living this empty existence?

I was abruptly confronted with my loneliness. The song pointedly proclaimed my inner aloneness... rootlessness... aimlessness... homelessness... friendlessness.... invisibility. I still had no passport or any other ID at this time, compounding my sense of anonymity.

Perhaps I had chosen that path; perhaps I'd been steered by childhood dysfunction, down the lonely road. Either way, it no longer seemed something desirable.

Taking hallucinogens can heighten or release existing emotions, and this moment, this encounter with Dylan's piercing question, confirmed semi-suppressed feelings beginning to surface from within.

Don't get me wrong. This LSD trip was not a religious revelation. I don't subscribe to George Harrison's description of his first acid trip, as the late Beatle recounted:

---

[43] Wings, *Band on the Run*, Apple, 1974.
[44] Bob Dylan, *Like a Rolling Stone*, Columbia, 1965: released almost prophetically the year I was born.

"The first time I took it, it just blew everything away. I had such an incredible feeling of well-being, that there was a God and I could see Him in every blade of grass".

Some ancient cultures and religions see the use of hallucinogens as a pathway to some kind of divine consciousness.

In contrast, I've come to see and experience God the Father as Love, who does not readily share space with our addictions and substances. After coming to a simple faith in Jesus a short time after this night in '87, the experience of being filled with the Holy Spirit eluded me until I was able to reach the point of desiring him above drugs and everything else.

When I finally reached that moment in 1989, the sense of being infused with his love and forgiveness left me with no desire to get stoned or drunk ever again.

Satisfaction comes in the shape of sacrificial love.

Back to '87...while my ingrained atheism was being seriously called into question, so also – during this acid trip in particular – were my feelings about my free, solitary lifestyle.

It was only a matter of weeks later, when my life turned from the anonymity of being a complete unknown to finding complete identity as a child of God, known to the Father, and found my direction home in more ways than one. How did that feel? Pretty damn good!

PART TWO:

COMING HOME

11: The first mile home

May you always know where the road home begins
and have the courage to walk the first mile.
Gerard Kelly – *The Prodigal Blessing*[45]

I'm glad I knew so little about church or Christianity back then. Like in any organisation, clique or culture, the jargon can be quite confusing. Churches talk a lot about "grace", i.e. how God's gift of Life through Jesus can only be accepted as a free gift by faith. They say there's nothing we can do to add to or take away from that gift, or from his love. And I believe it.

At the same time they often say, when someone has started out on the Christian life, that the person has "made a commitment", implying an onus on the individual to keep certain promises, rather than trusting in *God's* promises and following Jesus as best we can.

It's a mixed message.

What happens when that "commitment" waxes and wanes? Will we believe that God is still OK with us or will we beat ourselves up over our inevitable failures, remembering that that's (partly) why we needed Jesus in the first place?

Some years ago, I knew a couple who went to church several times and were very interested in becoming Christians, but didn't think they could ever "keep it up", as if being a Christian is about somehow making the

---

[45] Gerard Kelly, Spoken Worship: *Living Words for Personal and Public Prayer* (Grand Rapids: Zondervan, 2007).

grade. As far as I know, they never did come to that place of stepping forward into faith. Perhaps the role models in the church gave the impression of unachievably high standards. Or perhaps the couple had been misled by the idea of "making a commitment".

Sometimes, Christians use booklets to explain the ABC or ABCD (Admit, Believe, Confess... and something or other beginning with D) of becoming a Christian, as if the union between the complex personality of a unique human being and the Creator of this mysterious universe could somehow be reduced to a simple formula.

The New Testament presents no such formulas, nor does it ever speak of people making a commitment to Jesus. Each person's relationship to Jesus, or their conversion experience, is described quite uniquely. Where general terms are used, they tend to be phrases like "entered into life" or "followed Jesus".

Individual uniqueness, authenticity, the ability to be completely honest with God, especially about our weaknesses and failings, are essential ingredients to any life of faith. The whole thing is a journey of discovery, a learning process, through putting our trust in Jesus, and finding out what it means to walk personally, individually, with him.

Faith is more about placing our lives into his hands, leading to new life, than believing certain things with our heads (although some of that is important too) or dutifully committing to a religion.

Those early disciples, those fishermen and tax-collectors, started out following Jesus in their own stumbling way, fumbling and faltering, then gradually coming to new levels of love for him, for each other and other people, in response to his sacrificial love on the cross, most of them eventually willing to give up their lives for Jesus in return, such was his profound impact on them over years of being his followers – without ever losing their own unique personalities in the process.

Jesus often reiterated old Jewish prophecies like: "I desire mercy, not sacrifice," and opened them up in new ways. Time and again, for anyone who may have been confused about religion (and there were and are still many), he made no bones about it. He blew away all foolish pride and pretensions.

No, it's not about those noble things you might think, he said in effect, like duty and commitment or keeping the rules, which tend to breed arrogance. No, it's about humbling yourself enough to both *receive* mercy and to *show* mercy to people in any kind of physical, mental or spiritual need. Humbling yourself enough to show forgiveness, and to help out strangers.

A growing lifestyle of receiving and giving out tried and tested love.

The other day I briefly and happily helped a random stranger in the street who asked for help with carrying a piece of furniture from a shop to her car. Along the way I mentioned that I was a Christian. She said, somewhat despondently, "I try to be, but I'm not very good at it."

Admiring her humility, I almost replied in solidarity, "Me too", which would have been true but maybe not that helpful. Also, I've been learning not to try so hard, and *not to be too hard on myself*. Compassion starts with ourselves.

Just in time, I thought better of my response, saying instead, "You don't need to try too hard, you just need to let his love flow through you". I always like to pass on things I'm still learning myself...

I knew none of this in '87, though.

All I knew was that everything I'd heard and experienced pointed to the *probability* that God was real and that Christianity *seemed* to add up and make sense of the world.

During this period it felt so strongly like there was a tug of war going on for my soul. I'd been pulled between pursuing a Buddhist belief that everything was somehow "one" and questioning the very reality of the universe, and the more dualistic, Christian ideas that I'd been hearing: good and evil, God and Satan, truth and lie.

Although I came to embrace these Christian beliefs *and still do*, I've come to a less dualistic, certainly less black-and-white, faith in recent years, and would by no means dismiss Buddhist practices. More on that later.

It actually felt like maybe the devil was trying to draw me away from coming to faith in Jesus, while God was drawing me *towards* Christian faith.

Dr Micha Jazz, a spiritual writer for whom I have the greatest respect, says this about Satan:

> "Today to suggest that the devil might have a personality can raise an eyebrow or two. Many have reduced the title to little more than a metaphor for what lies behind all that's bad in our world. Such reductionism is dangerous..."[46]

I couldn't say exactly what I believe these days about the devil. I think beliefs (including mine) about such a personality are often confused and compromised by unhelpful medieval images of pitchforks and horns. But I do believe in a very real presence of evil in this world, which tries its

---

[46] Premier's *Voice of Hope* booklet, Issue 17.

damnedest to stop people from knowing their full, true identity and finding wholeness, *which is entirely what "salvation" is.*

"Satan", meaning adversary, is as good a name as any for this presence. And my very subjective experience in '87 of being pulled in two directions seemed to confirm the God/Satan ideas of Christianity.

The draw towards Jesus felt *almost* irresistible – not that God ever forces anyone to believe, and I understood that, even then – but I didn't *want* to resist any longer. It was a sweet call. And it really did feel like he was *calling* me to follow him.

I was 95% sure Christianity was true. The term "beyond reasonable doubt" sprang to mind.

I also knew there was no way of "proving" these things, and that the only possible way of closing or testing that 5% gap was through active faith – by putting it into practice. After sitting down and weighing it all up, some time around my 22nd birthday in Oct 1987, I prayed the first real prayer of my life:

"Well, God, I think I believe in you. I'm going to give this Christianity thing a try for a year or two and see what happens!"

Apparently, you're not "meant" to do that. But I did. And I'm so glad! I'm glad my first ever prayer was a genuine expression in my own individual, honest words. I'm glad I never went to church in that run-up to faith and wasn't led into repeating a set prayer of repentance or commitment. I'm glad I didn't make any promises I couldn't keep.

I'm glad that my stumbling attempts to follow Jesus in stages echoed those of his first disciples that we read about in the gospels, who also gave themselves to him in stages.

I'd love to say that it's always been about Jesus for me, but that wouldn't be entirely true. It started out as being about God and Christianity – this faith that made sense. As the years have gone on, Christianity has blurred more and more into the background, while Jesus, who alone satisfies my need for meaning, has come increasingly into focus.

I'm glad that my faith in God started out independent of church, so that through the ups and downs of faith, of life and especially of church life, my faith has rested securely in God, not in fallible leaders, who can rock the very core of our faith when they fail to meet our expectations if that faith is tied up with our allegiance to the organisation or community that we call church.

It's struck me that all my significant spiritual moments have taken place alone – a phenomenon I've come to recognise as an expression of my introvert personality.

I've discovered that God recognises my personality type and graciously meets with me on these terms.

Existentialist philosopher Paul Tillich described the difference between loneliness and solitude in this way:

> "Language... has created the word 'loneliness' to express the pain of being alone. And it has created the word 'solitude' to express the glory of being alone."

I find this a powerful statement about my own experiences of both kinds of aloneness.

To answer Dylan now about how it feels to be on my own, when proper solitude in my busy work-and-family-life is such a precious commodity, I concur with the sentiment of The Pretenders' recent ode to introversion, in which Chrissie Hynde describes being at her best on her own[47].

137

From being a lonely, insecure person desperately needing to be loved, alone in my atheist world, I can honestly say that over these last 3 decades since that very first day of stumbling faith I have *never* felt lonely, even during the 5 years I spent as a single man before meeting Janine, after making the decision to abstain from (even celibate) romantic relationships until I felt sure I'd met my future wife.

(This was perhaps a noble course of action; but also one rooted in insecurity and the fear of making a mistake. In any case, it all worked out for good in the end!)

Simultaneously, I've come to accept my love of solitude and have become less apologetic for being unsociable or quiet at times – for being "an introvert in a noisy, extrovert world", as Susan Cain puts it[48].

Today as I walked through my local park, I bumped into two wonderful, older ladies from my church struggling up the steep hill in the summer heat, one with a shopping-trolley-walking-aid. I slowed down to chat with these two women of faith whom I only knew a little, curious to get to know them better.

They asked me how long I'd been a Christian, and so after giving them a vague reply, I asked them the same question. Both of them gave me the exact date they'd been "born again".

"That's great," I thought, but I've never been able to specify a date because on that day I first prayed, I had no idea of the significance of the thing I'd just done. I had no idea I'd be changed forever, that my life

---

[47] The Pretenders, *Alone*, from the album *Alone*, BMG Rights Management, 2016.
[48] Susan Cain, *Quiet: The Power of Introverts in a World That Can't Stop Talking* (London: Penguin, 2013).

would take such a completely different path, although from day one it really did feel like a homecoming. Or at the very least, the first mile home. For the same reason, nor do I know the date of the second mile of my homecoming, which *did* take place in church. That first non-committal, solo prayer that kicked off my life as a new Christian was followed up a couple of weeks later, in a place that holds some of the fondest memories for me, with my second family.

12: California dreaming

...the ghettos of East LA, where young lives are ruined, still, by drugs, gangs and jail.[49]

Will I Am, singer

I don't know much about East Los Angeles, where my school friend Nancy was now living with her Aunt Eva, Uncle Danny and cousins Tony, Alfred and Terry, but my impression from my limited experience of the neighbourhood was of a safe, close-knit community, woven together by palpable love and faith.

For the second time on my travels round the States, this extraordinarily ordinary, humble, Mexican-American family embraced me as one of their own.

In fact, I'd been blessed by the family's hospitality on both sides of the Atlantic. In my teenage years, when my home was not home and Nancy was living in Lewes, her house would often be a haven, saving me from having to cycle the 11 miles back to Buxted in the middle of the night at the end of our parties and pub-crawls.

In the mornings I'd play Manic Miner and Monopoly with her brother David and other friends. Our only "additional" rule in Monopoly was that all cheating was allowed as long as you got away with it.

Nancy's mother Martha gave me my first taste of chilli con carne at this amazing house in Lewes in about 1982 – and I've been hooked ever since. In years to come, in certain circles I became known for my own

---

[49] Will I Am's description of his upbringing in East LA, in *The Big Issue* magazine.

homemade chilli con carne, laced with plenty of fresh chillies. Some like it hot. Others not.

I'm forever indebted to this family who showed me, from sixth form days onwards, what family could be, and "adopted" me as their own.

In East LA, so central was the local church, St Alphonsus, to this community, that it held FIVE services each Sunday, some in English, some in Spanish, to accommodate all its congregants. Here, it seemed, was a spiritual neighbourhood, with faith at its heart.

Highlights of my short time with this Catholic community included sampling a Mexican charity breakfast – probably the best breakfast I've ever had, comprising a stupendous combination of eggs, chillies and rice, spiced up with the magic ingredients of love and community.

During this week or two in East LA, I attended St Alphonsus Church. The service was modern, upbeat, with guitars and gusto. I'd never experienced church like this before. A far cry from what many associate with Catholicism.

But much more important than the style of service was this:

It was the first time I'd *ever* gone to church voluntarily.

I can't tell you how momentous – seminal, even – that moment was. At the end of the service I knelt in prayer for I don't know how long. Maybe 20 minutes. Maybe 5. Time was immaterial. Nor do I remember even a word of what I prayed, but it was from-the-heart and felt like a formalising of the try-it-and-see idea I'd initially voiced.

Thinking later about those days, the words of *California Dreamin'*[50] seemed to fit most aptly – especially as I scuffed through the autumn

---

[50] The Mamas & The Papas, *California Dreamin'*, Dunhill Records, 1965.

leaves of a New Jersey park that November, preparing to leave the USA for the last time, and pondered what life might have been like if I'd settled in LA as I'd vaguely considered.

The principal difference being that, unlike the subject in the Mamas & Papas classic, there was no falsehood (in fact, until recently, the line "I pretend to pray" I'd always misheard as "I began to pray") but a pure authenticity in this act of new faith in the LA church: a quiet, solo deed of genuine devotion, a second step in coming home to my true identity and the arms of my spiritual Father.

It's funny, but back then rebellion against the establishment often meant rebelling against the church and religion. I don't think the church has quite the same standing today, in terms of being seen as part of the "establishment" – a fact for which I'm very grateful.

Nowadays, I would guess young people seeking their own identity or going against the things of their fathers are more likely to be *apathetic* about the church. But back in the day, to align oneself with the church or Christianity was akin to joining the "establishment". Christianity was the last thing I ever thought I'd become part of.

Paradoxically, for that very reason, to become a Christian and start going to church felt like the ultimate rebellion, as I went against all expectations of anyone who knew me or dared to be different. It was rebellion against mainstream rebellion.

I was thinking for myself.

I like to think I've always tended to make up my own mind about things, rather than going with the flow of the masses, or even that of a subculture. Like any personality trait, independent-mindedness is often positive, but not *always*...

Positive qualities of individualism include innovativeness; creativity; and a pioneering spirit. The negative side is an inclination towards a wilful, even arrogant, disregard for the tried and tested wisdom and guidance of others. This is sometimes true of me.

Someone I know, who reminds me a bit of myself, describes herself as a "free thinker". I'm not convinced there really is such a thing. I may be judging unfairly, but she can be almost vitriolic online towards anyone with an opinion different from her own – chained to angry dogmatism, that doesn't look too much like freedom to me.

It makes it difficult for others, who aren't looking for a fight, to express disagreement, which means she loses some of her *freedom* to hear the thoughts of others. People who value independent thinking need to beware of arrogance, which serves only as a barrier to communication, learning, and therefore growth.

For me, free thinking includes freedom to show respect for people with different views and a willingness to listen.

So anyway, back to the story in hand...

Some weeks later, when I'd returned to England for reasons that I'll come to, word had got around Lewes that "Roger had got religion". My friend Scoby told me with a cheeky grin he'd expected to see me with a shaven head and an orange robe. I loved that. I found his comment hilariously comforting.

No one had expected me to become a *Christian*, of all things. Of course, the transition wasn't, in any way, a deliberate attempt to defy expectations. After all, it was a genuine discovery of faith. The shattering of stereotypes and presumptions was simply a delicious side-effect!

When I told other friends I'd "become a Christian", they said incredulously, "What were you before, then?" as if "Christian" was simply the religion of someone brought up in a white, western country: wasn't I already a Christian? No. I was never the sort of person to have obligingly ticked "C of E" on a medical form.

I found it hard at first to explain what I meant, that there had been an *internal* conversion from atheist to someone with a real, living faith. That I was no longer the same on the inside.

I'd had a genuine encounter with God, with faith – a spiritual awakening, which I could never turn my back on.

Nancy, who has also come to Christian faith since then, cementing our friendship even more deeply, had clearly spotted the difference, as she described to me:

> "I saw your life changed. You came to Los Angeles a couple of times to visit. I vividly recall one visit and you were markedly different. You had hope, you seemed alive in a way you weren't before. As someone who hadn't accepted Christ for myself (I believe He existed, I just didn't think I needed Him) it was a catalyst. I knew you as an atheist and now you most definitely were not an atheist!"

Not even the oppressive smog or the absurd wealth inequality of Los Angeles could ever dampen the eternal affection I have for East LA, home of my second homecoming step, nor for the Tellez family, so rich in love. I'm forever proud to be their adopted son and brother.

13: The hitch-hiker's guide to heaven

> *"There are plenty of aimless people on the road, all right. People who hitchhike from kicks to kicks, restlessly, searching for something: looking for America, as Jack Kerouac put it, or looking for themselves, or looking for some relation between America and themselves.*
>
> *But I'm not looking for anything. I've found something." "What is it that you've found?" "Hitchhiking."*
>
> Tom Robbins

When I first returned from America, forever changed by faith, I considered writing a book – it would be a melting-pot of anecdotes, adventures, the story of my conversion and hitch-hiking tips. After all, I had a fair bit of experience, having hitched roughly 25,000 miles over the two trips, by car, truck, train and even boat. It was to be called *The Hitch-Hiker's Guide to Heaven*.

I did use that title for a short personal testimony tract, which I used to give out prolifically in my former evangelical fervour. Not so much my style now, but it had its place.

Nearly 30 years later, I'm writing that book, though very different from the one that would have been written way back then. I'm a different person now, with a faith that's morphed with age.

Hitch-hiking is a dying art these days, but as a light-hearted nod to the "me" of 3 decades ago, here are my top 10 hitch-hiking tips, complete with UK and US road terms for people on both sides of the pond...

Top 10 Hitch-hiking Tips:

1. Always carry a marker pen. Writing your destination on a cardboard sign increases your chances of someone stopping – although your destination should be somewhere more realistic than Caracas if you're hitching out of a town in Scotland[51].

2. Never hitch in the rain – drivers hate the idea of wet people getting into their nice, comfy cars. Hitch-hiking was always much harder when it was raining, in both the UK and the USA.

3. Smile! ...even if you've been standing there for hours in the pouring rain (see 2). People are suspicious of hitch-hikers who look pitiful.

4. It always helps to have a pretty face with you. People are generally more likely to pick up a female than a male. Someone should start a firm: Rent-a-Female-Hitch-Hiker, for men who are hitching alone.

5. If you're in a city, you need to get to the city's edge, on to the freeway / main road, before trying to hitch a ride. Otherwise, drivers haven't a clue where you're going and won't stop – unless you're in a "dodgy" area of Detroit and some middle-class people decide they need to get you out of there fast.

---

[51] End scene in that lovable film, *Gregory's Girl*.

6. Stand at the start of a slip-road / on-ramp, so drivers have time to stop before getting to the freeway / motorway and avoid causing a pile-up.

7. Hiding all your worldly possessions in some bushes overnight by the freeway is a really dumbass thing to do.

8. If you spend any significant amount of time hitching in the States, you'll find yourself using words like "dumbass" – so much more expressive than "stupid".

9. Sleeping in the back of a pick-up truck or on a freight train as it travels through the night can be *really* cold! Don't expect to sleep.

10. Don't sleep out in American city parks. In the middle of the night you're likely to hear that dreaded sound: "Tsch-tsch-tsch..."of the sprinkler systems coming on, and you'll need to move FAST before you and all your stuff gets soaked. Happened to me more than once before I learned my lesson.

14: The point

If the point of life is the same as the point of a story, the point of life is character transformation. If I got any comfort as I set out on my first story, it was that in nearly every story, the protagonist is transformed. He's a jerk at the beginning and nice at the end, or a coward at the beginning and brave at the end. If the character doesn't change, the story hasn't happened yet.

Donald Miller

In a world tyrannised by cold, hard science, quantitative data and (often meaningless) numerical targets, there's been a welcome trend in academic quarters towards narrative research, which puts the *lived experience* of real people under the spotlight instead of inside the shadowy stats which they all too often inhabit – hidden by numbers. That means not only giving a voice to those who are seldom heard, such as people who are homeless or suffer mental health disorders, through the telling of first-hand life stories, but also examining and critiquing contemporary history, society and culture through the lenses of these narratives, enhanced by the individuals' own observations[52].

Warm, human subjectivity is given its rightful place of honour alongside the cold objectivity of traditional science.

Stories, whether myths, historical accounts, films, novels or biographies, have forever been the language of cultures, and a commentary on

---

[52] See, for example, the *Our Encounters With* series, published by PCCS Books.

societies. No more so than the stories of real people's lives. They are wondrously rich sources, on so many levels, of information and meaning. I'm been privileged to take part in a small pilot narrative research project, interviewing homeless or ex-homeless people, to elicit their life stories. Such projects aim to help the subjects make sense of their own lives, as well as informing researchers and their readers about a particular subject – in our case, the complex chains of events that led to these individuals' homelessness, and the part that hope and meaning play, if any, in their lives.

I've personally interviewed just two homeless men (whom we'll call Jim and Alex). Although there no legitimate generalisations to be formed, there are some notable observations to be made...

Jim, a reflective, disabled man in his 60s, tossed and turned over the years by alcohol misuse, anger and a string of losses and bereavements – most pertinently, the distress and guilt of having his dog put down, reported having had a faith in God for a long time. He spoke movingly of a psychological turning point that had happened when he forgave his father.

I first met Jim when he was transient and living in a tent. By the time we did the interview about a year later, he was sober and had settled into supported housing.

When asked what gave his life meaning, he talked of opportunities to help others in similar situations, as he'd already begun to do as a peer leader within a local charity.

Of course, he still has his struggles – don't we all? But Jim has been a success story, and he knows it. I don't mean he's arrogant – far from it – but in an entirely deserved and humble way he's proud of his progress.

Looking back, seeing the strides forward he's taken, and hearing the cheers of acclamation from friends and professionals reinforces Jim's own story and motivates him onwards on the same path.

Jim's story is full of hope, purpose and positive change. When thinking about his faith, forgiveness, recovery, and sense of purpose, it's hard, perhaps, to identify an order to this virtuous circle of events. Did his faith give him the courage to forgive his father? Was faith reinforced by the peace he found with his father? Why did he manage to settle into housing and sobriety at this particular moment in his life? Was it a sense of purpose that enabled Jim to resettle, or was it the other way round: did his near-miraculous resettlement instil in Jim a new sense of purpose? These are rhetorical, chicken-and-egg questions, but it seems to me that at the heart of his story, from way back, was an inner sense of positive spirituality that generated faith and forgiveness, driving Jim forward, at first tacitly, then later more overtly, towards recovery.

In contrast, the much younger Alex, in his late 20s, living in supported accommodation at the time of the interview and making a steady transition out of a lifestyle of drug use and homelessness, when asked, was unable to identify a single source of meaning or purpose in his life. Even his estranged baby son, whom he loved and missed, did not seem to spring to mind as an object of hope or purpose, until prompted by me, the interviewer.

In the ensuing 2 years after the interview, Alex spiralled downwards into a seemingly intractable abyss of depression and entrenched street homelessness. Although a number of external factors could be cited for Alex's reversal of fortunes, I can't help but think that his lack of apparent meaning and purpose – not being able to see any future for himself – lay at the heart of his decline.

Viktor Frankl, in describing the psychological state of fellow concentration camp prisoners, explained that

> "The prisoner who had lost faith in the future – his future – was doomed. With his loss of belief in the future, he also lost his spiritual hold; he let himself decline and became subject to mental and physical decay."[53]

I believe, however, in the actualising tendency of human beings that Carl Rogers wrote about – in a constructive future for someone with Alex's positive qualities, even if he's unable to see his own way forward just yet. I remain optimistic that, in time, with the right encouragement and opportunities and the grace of God, Alex will develop the kind of reflective and purposeful qualities demonstrated by Jim, that might enable him to envisage a future for himself, and move towards that future of hope and recovery.

A hope-full attitude is absolutely essential in workers like me, if we're to promote any sense of positive destiny for those who feel as if they are hope-less. We are advocates; we are "counsellors" in the broadest sense, called, paid, and/or positioned to bring out the best in people who have spiralled down to a place where they can't see any good for themselves. We are called to be harbingers of hope.

This is no false optimism. This is the impartation of unconditional, non-judgmental support and trust, which has the power to nurture the hope-

---

[53] Viktor Frankl, *Man's Search for Meaning*, (London: Rider, 2004), p.82.

less individual's self-worth and thereby the belief that things *can actually change*.

Hope is not just a vague aspiration, but an empowering force for self-belief and personal progress.

This role of advocate / counsellor / strengthener is also, interestingly, exactly what is meant by the Greek word *paraclete*, a description given by Jesus, of the Holy Spirit. Christians like me have this incredible unseen companion who does indeed bring out the best in us, inspires hope and gives us confidence for the future.

Which means that even in the darkest, most difficult times, when it's hard to see through the fog of our own confusion, we're still able to hold on to the sure knowledge that good will come out of it all. We're not immune to disappointment, anxiety, worry, stress and even depression, and yet...we're still able to retain a sense of positive future in the midst of painful emotions and unfathomable circumstances, as the Holy Spirit, the *paraclete*, the counsellor, whispers hints of hope into our hurting hearts. That has certainly been my experience.

Which in turn means that those who have had this experience of the Holy Spirit's comfort should be better placed than others to inspire others with hope.

Furthermore, Christian hope is rooted in *love*. That passage about love[54], famously recited at weddings, gives us this exhortation: "Love always trusts, always hopes, always perseveres."

That soul infusion of the Father's love energises us to care deeply with a love that believes the best for the hurting, the vulnerable and the

---

[54] 1 Corinthians 13, *The Bible.*

marginalised; love that sees their potential, recognises their immeasurable worth and doesn't give up on them.

And no wonder – it's the same love that the Father has shown to us; to me. I believe in the kind of Father that Jesus portrayed in his story of the wayward son who took to the road and squandered everything. Jesus revealed God as a parent who watches and waits expectantly for his children, longing for us even more than our souls long for him, welcoming us at the slightest hint of our return.

You could say that Christianity is all about homecomings. For me, to find faith was to embark on a series of homecomings: to God, to faith, to myself, to peace of mind, to my home country, to my destiny, career and calling. I was the prodigal who'd somehow found his way home to the Father's embrace.

I was profoundly moved by *The Return of the Prodigal Son* by Henri Nouwen, who in turn had been deeply moved by a Rembrandt painting of the same name. Nouwen summarises his series of reflections on the parable and the painting in this way:

> "The parable of the prodigal son is a story that speaks about a love that existed before any rejection was possible and that will still be there after all rejections have taken place. It is the first and everlasting love of a God who is Father as well as Mother. It is the fountain of all true human love, even the most limited. Jesus' whole life and preaching had only one aim: to reveal this inexhaustible, unlimited motherly and fatherly love of his God and to show the way to let that love guide every part of our daily lives. In his painting of the father, Rembrandt offers me a glimpse of

that love. It is this love that always welcomes home and always wants to celebrate."[55]

This is the love that can guide and inspire hope in us for every wayward or broken individual – ourselves and others.

This is the love and hope that lie at the heart of many Christian social action projects, but also at the heart of many non-religious organisations and individuals who, with or without faith, nevertheless operate with the energy of this Universal, Divine love.

And I trust and hope that this is true of me.

Back to our two friends and their polarised interviews...

Jim and Alex are friends and have been a support to each other. Maybe something of Jim will eventually rub off on Alex. Maybe reflectivity will grow with age. But for now, the two men's lives stand in stark contrast.

Meaning and purpose lie at the heart of my story, too. Purpose in life is one of the biggest changes that transpired within my own faith-fuelled transformation.

Master illusionist and atheist Derren Brown says that humans are "story-forming" creatures, and that the story we believe *about ourselves* is what matters.

It's certainly true that we tend to become defined, for better or worse, by the stories we tell about ourselves, whether to others or within that internal, often *infernally negative*, dialogue. And I can see how Jim's belief in his own positive story has helped to perpetuate his progress.

I've told my conversion story a number of times in various ways, to individuals, to groups and churches, and in writing. It's benefitted me at

---

[55] Henri J.M. Nouwen, *The Return of the Prodigal Son* (London: Darton, Longman & Todd, 1994).

least as much as others, in helping to reinforce the positive changes that resulted from finding faith.

Writing this book has been an inevitable catalyst of catharsis and has opened my eyes still wider to the endless grace I've received.

Telling my story fosters my own faith and rekindles surprised delight. The story I believe about myself does matter – Brown's right.

But the constant rippling outward change in my life – the visible metamorphosis from an initial, hidden rebirth of this pupa – began radically and dramatically as a result of coming to faith in Christ and *his* story, rather than by believing any story of my own.

I described earlier the life-changing impact the Sermon on the Mount had on me as a young atheist. It's said, in that part of the Bible, that Jesus came across as someone completely different from any of the other religious teachers of the time – that he spoke with *authority*.

Thank goodness, speaking as a typical, independent bloke who resists being told what to do, that doesn't mean he preached in a domineering, lording-it-over-the masses kind of way.

Authority here is related to the word *author*, meaning Jesus knew what he was talking about, because he was the *author* (originator) of his own teachings.

From that encounter with Jesus' words in the Sermon on the Mount in '86, through my travels in the States, through the transition into faith, and into the last 30 years as a reformed, reforming person, it could be said that Jesus has been the *author* of this story too.

Perhaps it would be more accurate to say co-author.

External/internal locus of control is a psychological term referring to the extent to which people see their lives as determined by external forces (other people, luck, fate, God, or "the system", for example) or by their own (internal) decisions.

My locus of control seems, if anything, to swing more towards the internal end of the spectrum, evidenced by both a self-directed nature and a tendency to blame myself rather than others when things go wrong. Faith in God seems to have engendered in me an acute sense of responsibility and self-determination. I don't feel like a puppet on God's strings or anyone else's.

At the same time, and paradoxically, I share a sense with many other people of faith that "my days are written in his book", as King David wrote in the Psalms. A sense that, from a human, finite, time-bound perspective, God changed the storyline and has co-written, with me, a new life. And yet, that from an eternal viewpoint, the new story was always meant to be.

I believe that "my" story is also Jesus' story – a message from him to others.

The immediate changes that took place in my life were, quite literally, overnight and miraculous. There was a revolutionary moment, a coup de soul, where what was no longer was. Where what was to be suddenly was.

Later changes developed gradually and in stages, as they do for anyone with any measure of reflectivity, self-awareness or spiritual faith.

I guess I'd say that I've made sense of my story, as the years have gone by, through the practice of my faith: in prayer, spiritual reading, my career as a nurse, my encounters with hidden beauty in the faces of the homeless, and in all the various expressions of church. You could even say that for me as a Christian, "making sense of my story" is equivalent to "working out my salvation" – a Biblical phrase to describe the ongoing process of change rippling out from the central miracle.

This enduring transition began as a sudden, fundamental inner revolution, central to my soul, my mind, my very personhood, the likes of which I have rarely, if ever, seen in anyone other than those who turn to Jesus. I've seen individuals improve, progress, and overcome obstacles and addictions. But when a person finds Christ, or is found by him, she or he is no longer the person they were. Their fundamental motivation and desires change in an instant. At least, that was my experience, as witnessed by Nancy and recalled in her words in the last chapter.

The inner transformation as a result of Christian faith is so immediate and radical for many people that it defies being explained away as simply a result of believing our own stories or growing up. No wonder they sometimes call it being "born again" or born of the Holy Spirit – an expression coined by Jesus himself, who told a Jewish leader: "Unless you are born again, you cannot see the kingdom of God."

For many years, like other Christians, I thought that this was really just another term for becoming a Christian. I recoiled at the expression "born-again Christian", because *what other kind of Christian is there*?

Some of those early years of faith were monochrome days of evangelical zeal, influenced in part by the church I was with, that left little room for subtle shades of life or the wondrous joy of unknowing. Nowadays, you could say that my faith is increasingly rainbow-coloured. Far more compelling, I think.

An alternative view of this important statement about being "born again" is captured appealingly by Baptist minister Chuck Queen on the progressive Christian blogsite, Patheos:

"One can think of being born again as a clearing away of all the debris and obstacles so that the dynamic energy, love, compassion, and nonviolent power of God (the Spirit) can flow unhindered in us and through us into the world...

Our job is to get rid of the clutter that dams up the flow of living water. So if we want to know and share in the aliveness of God then our pride, prejudice, resentment, hate, and lack of forgiveness will have to go...

It we do this once, we will have to do this a thousand times...

If someone should ask me: 'Have you been born again?' I will say: 'Yes, I have been born again...and again and again and again. And tomorrow? Yes, I will once again need to be born again.'"[56]

Whether or not Jesus intended this kind of interpretation, I love Queen's explanation, I relate to it *experientially*, and find it immensely reassuring for the non-religious world around me. After all, there are countless people who wouldn't call themselves "Christian" and are utterly repelled from religion by their conception and experiences of so-called Christianity, and yet "see" and promote the kingdom of God, as described by Jesus and the Bible writers in terms of justice, mercy, forgiveness, nonviolent resistance, personal wholeness and societal peace.

At the same time, I also identify entirely with the idea of experiencing a complete new life at the moment of conversion.

Like a lot of ambiguous ideas and statements in the Bible with hints of paradox and double meanings, I'll accept *both/and*, rather than *either/or*.

---

[56] Queen, C. *Being born again in Unfundamentalist Fashion.* http://www.patheos.com/blogs/unfundamentalistchristians/2015/06/being-born-again-in-unfundamentalist-fashion/

Yes, I was born again in '87. Yes, I will continue to be born again, that I might increasingly encounter social justice and mercy unfolding from within and around me.

After all, when we're talking about the kingdom of God and spiritual matters, how can there not be an element of mystery and *vastness* beyond our human understanding?

There's a Jewish saying that the God who is small enough for my mind to comprehend is too small for my heart to feel that I am loved.

***

Many years later, after I'd trained as a nurse and was working nights in a nursing home, I worked with Bernice, a sweet, older West Indian lady with whom I got on well and who attended a Seventh Day Adventist church. One night, as we were chatting, she asked me whether I was "religious". Now, to me, "religious" has always been a dirty word, in both my pre-Christian and Christian days, suggesting adherence to external rules and rituals rather than living in the love of God. This had been instilled in me from the start. Even before stepping into faith, I remember Ray Galloway telling me he wasn't "religious" – that Christianity wasn't a "religion", because it's not about us trying to fulfil certain duties to appease a distant deity, but accepting a free gift from the God who comes close.

Many Christians shy away from being thought of as "religious", with so many negative connotations to the word, preferring to describe themselves as "spiritual".

In fact, a few years ago I initiated and organised a church event entitled "Religion is dead – Jesus is alive!"

So I hesitated to reply to Bernice's question. However, knowing she was also a Christian and therefore feeling no particular fear of potential conflict, I simply replied, "Well, I'm a *Christian*."

Bernice persisted, "But are you *religious*?"

My curiosity now piqued, I asked her what she meant by "religious".

Her reply took me by surprise: "Well, I don't drink, I don't smoke, I don't swear..."

By now I'd been a Christian for a number of years and didn't think *any* Christians defined religion in those terms. Perhaps these were the things that were important to the Seventh Day Adventist Church, of which I knew very little.

The word "religion" scarcely gets a mention in the Bible. Where it is used, it's generally used to contrast "false", hypocritical and negative religion that emphasises external adherence to rules with the "true" religion of a renewed heart that expresses care and advocacy for those experiencing poverty or marginalisation.

In fact, earlier this year, I told a Christian friend, "I probably need to swear more."

I'll just let that last statement sink in. Yes, I did say I probably need to swear *more*, not less.

This friend, like me, works in a public service. Andy tells me that his workplace is a bit of a rowdy, macho environment, and as a Christian it can be hard not to get drawn into some of their ungodly ways...like swearing.

It only took a moment of brief reflection on my part to reply that, in my own work situation, I find it more important, in terms of demonstrating my faith, to avoid colluding with others in negative behaviour like speaking critically about colleagues, and to ensure I'm consistent in treating clients with value and holism rather than as problems to be solved – a mindset that so easily creeps into an environment of high stress and complex needs. To be distinctive as a Christian, for me, means above all integrity, genuineness and care for others.

I explained that, personally, I don't find it difficult not to swear.

When I became a Christian, swearing and blaspheming disappeared from my repertoire of speech pretty much overnight. Blaspheming especially. When Jesus (or God) is real to a person, it seems unthinkable to use his name as a swear word, just as I wouldn't dream of doing so with my wife's name.

Using other swear words seemed to stop instinctively, too. Maybe it just seemed like the "Christian thing to do". Or perhaps a desire to speak positive, up-building words rather than negative, potentially offensive words developed out of an intuitive, new, deep sense of respect for other people.

People take on a whole new value when Christ enters a person's heart. I remember an old friend saying that when he became a Christian, he started "noticing people" more. Self-centredness gets replaced progressively by an awareness of and concern for others. I guess that's a big reason why Christians tend not to swear too much.

For the Christian, authentic love for God is inseparable from a genuine valuing of people.

But when Andy spoke of avoiding swearing at work, I retorted that I probably need to swear *more* – in conversation with clients, at least.

On the one hand, the therapeutic relationship between nurse / health care worker and client requires genuineness, so deliberately swearing, contrary to normally "clean" speech, could be seen as putting on a false front.

On the other hand, as a nurse, I already tend to tailor my approach to the client / patient, depending on their personality, circumstances and any existing relationship I have with them. That flexible, individualised approach is a standard interpersonal skill required on the part of any health or social care professional, in order to build rapport, develop empathy and provide optimal care and support.

What would Jesus do? I think he would swear with those who swear, in order to melt barriers, forge connections and make the kingdom of God go viral.

To use a different example, I was at a multiagency meeting where I was (not shocked but) surprised to hear a mental health colleague use the F-word in a discussion about a vulnerable client of his. It was such an unusual thing to hear in the context of a professional meeting that at first I thought he was quoting someone else.

Then I realised the momentary swearing had sprung as a reflex out of the justified anger and frustration this colleague had felt over a seemingly impossible situation in which a vulnerable older lady was at risk of death because of inflexible systems. He was right to feel the way he did. He was right to express his concern the way he did. I doubt anyone was offended in the context. Would Jesus have sworn in the same situation over apparent injustice and system failures? Quite possibly.

And I mention the case of swearing as an example of how, for me and for other Christians, external, behavioural changes like smoking, drinking and swearing are almost incidental – peripheral indicators of a deeper renewal, like the slow, steady radial pulse of a man who's undergone heart surgery.

At the risk of stating the obvious, being a Christian, even being "religious" in the true sense, is never about external, potentially misleading signs like whether we drink, smoke or swear, but about much deeper heart change. The point of my story is homecoming, not of turning over a new leaf, or even "recovery". Not even of simply becoming a better person, although that was true too.

My soul had found its home in God, and in that home was a new life, a new person, a new story. A story of identity, belonging, purpose, and new character.

This is where the new story begins.

15: Manic street preachers

Your Love Alone Is Not Enough
Manic Street Preachers[57]

It was one of the scariest Christian moments I've encountered. I use the word "Christian" loosely.

Jason (we'll call him) marched out from the mixed gaggle of the church that had gathered to "bless" the people of the sleepy Sussex town with our well-meaning efforts to spread the good news of Jesus. He sounded *angry*, as he addressed the minding-their-own-business shoppers around him.

"**REPENT!! REPENT!!**" ROARED JASON AT THE TOP OF HIS VOICE at the poor, cowering, innocent passers-by in the shopping precinct that Saturday morning in the early 1990s. Even for this church, with its somewhat in-yer-face approach, it was bolder than bold. Brasher than brash.

Many of us laughed nervously at our friend's unorthodox style, unsure whether to admire or cringe, or kneel in repentance ourselves. I think Jason was trying to emulate John the Baptist. I wonder what he thinks of that tirade now, more than 25 years later, or if he remembers it. To be fair, many of us were still finding our way in expressing that instinctive urge to share our faith.

He toned down the rest of his talk – a bit, but I'll never forget that manic street preacher's urgent, opening call to "**REPENT!!**"

---

[57] Manic Street Preachers, *Your Love Alone Is Not Enough*, Columbia, 2007.

***

A couple of years earlier, I'd been in a church in Brighton, receiving prayer after the service for some struggles I was going through as a new Christian, in which I was making ambivalent, half-hearted efforts to quit cannabis.

The young, sincere man supporting me in prayer gently questioned me about my initial conversion experience and whether I'd "repented" at the time – because Christian conversion is generally thought to involve a twofold process of *faith* and *repentance*. Had I simply come to believe, or had I *also* intentionally turned away from my sins?

It wasn't a bad question by any means, but religious terminology was still so new to me, so I asked him to clarify. "What do you mean by 'repent'?" To him and to many others in churches, becoming a Christian involves actively turning away from all identifiable sins in one's life – while at the same time recognising that this will be an ongoing lifetime process for which we'll need the Holy Spirit's help.

Had I repented in this sense? Well, certainly not as consciously or formally as that, because I'd come to faith in my own individual way, in solitude, with no religious formula or external prompting. As mentioned earlier, now in my much older and maybe wiser years, I'm very glad to have had the kind of "conversion" I had, because the whole thing was so utterly *genuine*, and perhaps set me up for the lasting, authentic, faith that I think I have.

In fact, after I'd been sharing openly with a friend about my newfound faith on my return to the UK, she commented to me, "You're so real!" It was such a warm compliment that I've never forgotten it. No pretence about my faith or my ongoing struggles, doubts and faults. No fake claims. I've always wanted, though at times failed, to retain that realness.

But encounters like this one, with the young, praying companion in church, made me question at times the veracity or depth of my conversion. Had I truly repented?

***

Good psychology is essential in my line of work, in supporting people with complex needs.

Therapeutic techniques and theories such as Prochaska and DiClemente's Cycle of Change, motivational interviewing, person-centred counselling and cognitive behaviour therapy, for example, all emphasise the reality that genuine, lasting behaviour change generally springs out of an individual's own inner qualities, resources, and sense of purpose – that people don't often change simply in response to external pressure – although other people such as the counsellor, pastor or friend can help the person to tap into his/her own internal resources through those approaches.

If you've ever had a partner or family member who's tried to nag you into quitting smoking / drinking or dieting, for example, you'll know that that pressure is more likely to reinforce the behaviour than to empower you to quit.

Being told to repent or to stop doing this or that is unlikely to help very much. The Bible contains much good psychology and makes it abundantly clear that commandments on their own can never change a person's heart, but believing and experiencing the sacrificial love of Jesus can. According to the Bible, grace (love, freely given) is the great motivator.

Church psychology, on the other hand, is not always so well-informed. There can be huge pressure to conform, to "repent", to do or believe certain things. Churchgoers may acquiesce out of loyalty, fear or guilt, which are not *always* poor motivators but, without questioning, reflecting and forming their own informed decisions, can lead to unhealthy emotional patterns, a dry sense of duty, and even incongruence, that is, a mismatch between values and actions, amounting to hypocrisy.

While out shopping one day, my attention was grabbed by the slogan I spotted on a small girl's T-shirt: "I totally agree with myself"!

I was immediately struck by the sheer profundity of that ostensibly self-centred statement, and couldn't help but wonder how many shoppers walking past the girl missed its significance.

To totally agree with oneself is a *noble* aim – to reach that place where one's values and actions perfectly line up. A place of absolute integrity. I know one Person, at least, who lived that dream.

Churches (and other groups) that encourage individuality and diversity of thought help their members to become more fully human, more fully themselves and, therefore (this may come as a surprise to some), more God-like.

Jesus was fully himself and, as well as being fully God, was fully human, which is almost not that different! Full humanity mirrors the human's Maker.

Unfortunately, I've experienced situations where conformity of thought is so prized that human-ness is squashed, thus wiping away God's messy, living fingerprints, settling instead for bland, sterile fakery and boring homogeneity.

However, I'm chuffed also to have been in churches where individuality is allowed to flourish, even fostered, thereby revealing the manifold wonders of God through the diversity of his people.

At least that's my view, on which I totally agree with myself!

***

There seems to be a rich and wise tradition that recognises and indeed celebrates the overlap between psychology and meditative spirituality. Contemplative authors like Thomas Merton and Richard Rohr draw deeply on the learning of tried and tested psychology in their writings.

The Bible, too, includes a wealth of wisdom on the transformation of hearts, minds and behaviour through mindfulness, finding inner strength through meditation, and even the companionship of God in contemplation.

For years, I was bemused by the apostle Paul's claim that, as a result of meditating on all that's good and pure and beautiful, and then reflecting this in our lives, the *God of peace* [rather than the *peace of God*] will be with us.[58] I would expect peace to emanate from meditative practices. But that was not Paul's statement.

It's taken me a long time, and a quantum step into contemplation, to know experientially what he meant. Our stillness, our active meditation on the character and truths of God, actually makes space in our experience, in our very being, for the reality of eternal Yahweh, the *compassionate presence* of our Abba Father. No wonder contemplatives like the late Brennan Manning could eulogise with such exuberance about

---

[58] Philippians 4, The Bible.

the furious love of God and how he loves us so much more than we do ourselves.

In Christian meditation, we come face to face with both Abba and ourselves. In that interface, we discover the doleful discrepancy between his compassion for us and our own heretical self-hatred. In the place of stillness, we *begin* to learn to love ourselves as he loves us, and reflect that same glorious love out to others.

Which then makes sense of the fact that, when the Bible speaks of contemplating God's glory, the phrase has the dual meaning of *reflecting* that glory.

Modern stress management and counselling practices embrace meditative and mindful approaches, which are not necessarily "spiritual" or "religious" in and of themselves, but which nevertheless have their roots chiefly in spiritual (e.g. Buddhist and ancient Christian) traditions. To thinking people of faith, it comes as no surprise that Christian spirituality is inherent in many other spheres of life, not merely in religion, believing as we do that our God, Yahweh, is the great Neuro-psychologist who designed our minds and pervades our world with his presence.

God is, of course, not religious – he has no need to be!

Such a shame, then, that many branches of the modern church seem to have lost this wisdom – while, happily, those traditions that draw on ancient Christianity still drink deeply of these waters of life.

And that, as Forrest Gump would say, is all I have to say about that.

At least for now...

***

True repentance, genuine change, must come from within. And it took me a long time to realise that, although in those early years I sometimes doubted the depth of my conversion because I didn't yet conform (and maybe still don't!) to the church's "rules", actually the most momentous repentance had already taken place within.

With newfound faith came an immediate motivation to do something practically useful with all I had. An acute awareness transpired, right from the start, of the gifts I'd been given *by God*, as I now recognised: intelligence (albeit with the limitations described earlier), excellent health, a sheer abundance of energy, enough O-levels to get by, and now on top of all that, a spiritual awakening. I had so much to *give*!

All at once, I no longer had any desire or need to live for sex, drugs & travel, but a burning, yearning desire to put all that I'd been given to good use, to help others in need, in some way.

I didn't know that Jesus said, "Freely you received; now freely give."

I didn't know of Jesus' parable that suggests a responsibility to "invest" our talents wisely.

The idea was there in my belly, in my bones. I've sometimes been asked if I see myself as "giving something back" to society. My reply is that rather than giving back, I'm giving *out* what God has placed inside me, letting his love flow through me like a river.

In discussing *metanoiete*, the New Testament Greek word for repentance, Shaun Lambert, the "Benedictine Baptist", explains:

> "What emerges is not habitual, rule-bound patterns of thought and behaviour but an inner freedom that swims in the dynamic love of God for the world and its peoples."[59]

Such a fitting description of my own experience.

---

[59] Shaun Lambert, *A Book of Sparks* (Watford: Instant Apostle, 2014), p.38.

Ideas about returning to the UK to make a difference to people struggling with poverty and disaffectedness flooded my head; simultaneously, thoughts of doing charity work in a third world African country were emerging.

I experienced a startlingly immediate and pressing inclination towards a combination of practical and spiritual help. Holistic care began as a vague but definite aim. Astoundingly, 30 years later, that hasn't changed one iota. It's as if God himself branded this calling on to my very soul. He did. Even now, I can scarcely believe the magnitude of the metamorphosis – a 180-degree revolution from atheist to believer, from hedonist to giver. How did I ever doubt my conversion?

One dictionary defines the English word *repent* as: *to turn from sin and dedicate oneself to the amendment of one's life.* Both *repentance* and its Greek counterpart in the Bible, *metanoia,* carry with them the idea of changing one's mind and life direction – a new way of thinking, leading to new action. A perfect way to describe what happened to me.

I had certainly, definitely, without a doubt, *repented* – intuitively, unwittingly. Not through any external teaching or pressure, not because anyone had told me what to do to become a Christian.

It just happened, as a work of the Spirit within me – a *gift* of the Holy Spirit.

I didn't know, I *didn't need* to know, that the Bible says: "He who steals must steal no longer, but find something useful to do with his hands." I didn't consciously "repent" of shoplifting, or think: "now I'm a Christian, I should do something useful." It never crossed my mind to steal again, nor did I particularly realise at first that I'd stopped doing it. It just happened. It dawned on me later that I was living what the Bible taught.

Likewise, after returning to England and its pubs, it took me a while to realise I was no longer chucking all my money into fruit machines as I used to. That addiction, for one, was forever broken, never to return.

And the point of explaining the sheer instinctiveness of these changes is my attempt to represent Christianity as the spiritual revolution that I believe it is and to bust misconceptions about it being a life of following rules or "living by the book". As much as I love and treasure the Bible as a source of hope, guidance, wisdom, and above all a signpost to Jesus – to be a Christian, I believe, is to live out that inner revolution of love that springs from faith.

As one of the Bible writers himself (St Paul) put it: "The only thing that counts is accepting the infallibility of the Bible and following it literally and rigidly."

Not really – of course not. There's nothing like that invention of man-made religion in the Bible. Instead, Paul gave this wonderful, basic tenet of wisdom:

"The only thing that counts is faith expressing itself through love."

Couldn't have put it better myself!

There are some who say that becoming a Christian is really *all* a step of faith, not a twofold step of faith and repentance; they would say that to cite repentance as a condition of receiving unconditional love is oxymoronic, if not moronic, and makes a mockery of the whole Christian idea of grace being a free gift.

I'd go along with that entirely.

God is love, the great psychologist and inner motivator, our co-collaborator driving positive hope and behaviour change from the inside out. Or as Jesus put it, "Whoever has been forgiven much loves much."

Right from the start, I had a huge feeling of being forgiven for all my "stuff", of being loved from above, and of that forgiveness driving a deep desire in me to love others in practical ways with all that God had given me. **Because love always looks outwards.**

Irvin Yalom, writing about the therapeutic relationship between psychotherapist and patient in "Love's Executioner", sets forth his triplicate mantra:

> "It's the relationship that heals; it's the relationship that heals; it's the relationship that heals."[60]

I can't argue with that – even though Yalom writes from an atheist, existentialist, and humanistic point-of-view. The one common denominator between hundreds of schools of counselling and psychotherapy is the importance of the relationship between therapist and patient.

Positive, loving relationships in any context, whether professional or personal, are a source of healing. However, as much as I advocate counselling and other psychological therapies, human support alone is not enough to meet the deepest human needs.

Which is one reason why I believe that those who are most broken, with the most complex needs, as many homeless people are, need (more than most people) much more than human support.

As the Manic Street Preachers – not "Jason", but that most excellent band from Wales – sang about a very human experience:

> *Your Love Alone Is Not Enough.*

---

[60] Irvin Yalom, *Love's Executioner* (London: Penguin, 1991).

Don't get me wrong: human support is *absolutely essential* too. And miraculously, human love and support can be a true conduit for divine love. The Father, who is Love, often reveals himself through his children. Most people who have experienced abuse, rejection and trauma at the hands of others, as so many homeless people have, need to experience the opposite of that trauma: unconditional love, acceptance, genuineness, trustworthiness – from other adults, in order to restore their faith in human beings, before they can ever begin to believe that there is an even greater, divine love to be received and embraced. Divine love that offers the deep, liberating healing and forgiveness.

They may not call this love "God" or "Jesus" – these are just names. Jesus is greater than his name or the ideas that people have about him. His love is able to reach the deepest depths of a person's heart, and when someone with complex needs receives this healing love – this ultimate relationship that heals – s/he has perhaps found Jesus – albeit sometimes by another name.

This is another reason why 12-step programmes can work so well. Someone may trust in a higher power, not even knowing who or what that higher power is, but in the process receive the healing love of Jesus – unwittingly!

Of course, like anyone, I'm still learning to love. A lifetime is too short for broken human beings to learn how to love like God does. But that journey from self-centredness to love was clearly begun that autumn of '87 as I made my way out of Oregon, to California, and then back to England. Repentance had most definitely begun.

When faith is real, change *will* follow. It's virtually impossible not to "repent" once love has made its home in a person's heart and shown that person forgiveness and a new way of living – when love has started to show them all that they can be.

It doesn't of course mean overnight perfection, but a visible change of direction. In my case, that was true literally, geographically, as well as spiritually and morally.

The spiritual homelessness that lay behind my itinerant lifestyle choice was cured forever in a moment, and I made for LA, not only to see Nancy (the occasion when she witnessed those early signs of life change recalled in the quote given earlier, and I made my first-ever voluntary church attendance, at St Alphonsus), but also to pay a visit to the British Consulate to obtain a temporary passport so I could return to England. My visit to the Consulate was the last incident of being disbelieved that I encountered in my transient life – the final act of dealing with the loss of all my possessions in those bushes a couple of months earlier. I guess they suspected me of having sold my passport for a bag of weed or something. I often see homeless people who have lost possessions, sleeping bags, important letters and documents, passports and birth certificates. It's easy to judge or disbelieve or make assumptions as to how they "lost" these things, but unwise actions, drug and alcohol use, theft, vulnerability, the instability and insecurity of living on the streets... all these factors make it near impossible for homeless people to hold on to their belongings.

I'm thankful for my own experiences that make it easier to show understanding towards people in these circumstances.

The Consulate officials finally agreed to issue me a temporary passport, and I prepared to journey back "home", that is, to England (more to follow on the new appeal of my home country).

My heart had found its home, its rest – in God. And as for those plans to hitch round the world, well, distant horizons had faded to grey.

Within weeks I was on a plane back to the UK to pursue a new life of purposeful giving in place of purposeless taking – which had detracted more from my own soul than from anyone or anything else. Altruism had taken root within, banishing meaninglessness to the distant past.

The old had gone, the new had irrevocably come.

16: Wonderful remark

We look at a picture of the Milky Way... People say it's 100 billion stars, and dust and gas and so on – but it also contains the everyday items and events that we experience here on earth – and there's an absurdity to that. That the universe, with all its majesty and extraordinary force, is in part here to create a packet of pickled onion Monster Munch.

Keith Tyson, artist

My first attempt at a book was in my mid-teens, when I got as far as writing a dozen pages of a comedy-fantasy-hippy, slightly science-fictiony, book of random, disconnected plots and non-plots, with fantasises of sex and marijuana[61]. A projection of my life goals of sex, drugs & itinerancy. It was teenage garbage.

I only ever showed it to one person – a friend at school – who seemed to like it and said my few pages bore a resemblance to *The Hitch-Hiker's Guide to the Galaxy*, which I'd heard of but never read. She suggested I continue to avoid the Douglas Adams classic and its potential influence, so as to keep my book's individuality.

Those ramblings were the first budding signs of a love of writing (which wasn't to emerge properly for about another 30 years) but also of a latent search for life's meaning (that was to become more blatant than latent a few years later).

---

[61] One curious fact about that book-attempt was that I included a fantasy involving a woman called Janine; then about 15 years later I met a real woman called Janine and married her! We've now celebrated over 20 years of marriage.

Despite many geeks' fascination with hidden meanings behind the late, great Douglas Adams' choice of 42 as the answer to the ultimate question of Life, the Universe and Everything, Adams himself stressed that he chose the number entirely at random, as a joke.

Nevertheless, his writings suggest that he, like many, grappled with life's meaning. A devout atheist, Adams confessed his fascination with religion, explaining that "I love to keep poking and prodding at it. I've thought about it so much over the years that that fascination is bound to spill over into my writing."

Existential psychology tells us there's an innate search for meaning in everyone. Existentialists, primarily of the atheist variety, claim that the *meaninglessness* of life is a "given" of human existence, and that it's up to each one of us to determine our own individual meaning to our existence. The meaning*less*ness of the universe is assumed by many, including my former, younger self, who wrote that essay for the school magazine, casting Sid Vicious as an iconic role model of the futility of life and the consequential call to anarchy!

Christian theologian and founder of existentialism, Soren Kierkegaard, pointed to Christian faith as the source of ultimate meaning; yet he too suggested that people need to discover their own subjective meaning. For many Christians, life's meaninglessness is entirely dispelled by the reality and purpose of their faith. I confess to being one of those. I say "confess", because to say that meaninglessness in my life has been eradicated by Jesus sounds like one of those trite, superficial answers religious people give to all of life's complex problems.

Like: "Just give your life to Jesus and everything will be fine." "Need peace? Get Jesus!" "Looking for meaning? Jesus is the answer!"

But hopefully you know by now that I'm not that kind of Christian. So allow me to unpack this a little:

So, these two middle-aged men walk into a coffee shop and start discussing the meaning of life...

Well, it sounds like a joke, so if you think of a punchline, let me know, but one recent mellow summer's morning there *were* in fact two middle-aged men, or Grumpy Old Gits (GOGs) as my friend Dave and I like to call ourselves, in a coffee shop, engaging in existential discourse...

That morning, as the two GOGs muse on Life, Theology and Everything over our misty Americanos, Dave discloses that, despite having been a Christian for many years, he struggles with meaninglessness. He tells me about the sorts of conversations he has with his wife, who doesn't share his internal conflict.

"Margaret says to me, 'Well, you find meaning when you help someone else, don't you?' And yes, I do, to an extent. But then, so what? What's the point in that meaning?"

I love our chats, me and Dave, the Grumpy Old Gits.

Dave emphasises that he's not depressed. "I have these conversations with Margaret about life's meaninglessness, then my thoughts turn to breakfast, and suddenly I'm: 'Ooh, we're having croissants! Great!'" he explains with genuine delight, "and everything's all right again."

Dave reminds me of a Peanuts cartoon in which Snoopy is lying face upwards on his kennel in his usual fashion, wrestling with the meaning of life, when Charlie Brown turns up with his supper dish. Snoopy jumps up, excitedly declaring, "AH! MEANING!!"

Dave gave me full permission to reproduce our conversation, including use of his real name. He's not ashamed to admit that, in spite of his long-established Christian faith, he finds himself in a state of existential uncertainty. Like me, he has a healthy, questioning attitude to faith and life, and doesn't placidly accept religious platitudes.

He and I had both recently read Richard Rohr's fantastic explanation of Franciscan spirituality, *Eager to Love,* and curiously (perhaps for different reasons) one particular paragraph out of the whole book had stood out for both of us:

> "The 'mystery of the cross' is *Paul's code-breaking and fundamental resolution for the confusing mystery of life!* Without it, it seems most people become cynics, depressed, bitter, or negative by the middle of life, because there is no meaning in the death of all things and the imperfection of everything. For Paul, the deepest level of *meaning* is ironically the deep, grace-activated acceptance of a certain *meaninglessness!* We are able to leave room for God to fill in the gaps, and even trust that God will! This new leap of logic is often called faith." [62]

That morning, as our Costa coffees cooled in our hands, our verbal meanderings were animated by this intriguing, even enigmatic, statement from the seasoned Franciscan friar. Is Rohr, a wise man steeped in Christian faith, suggesting that life is in some ways *actually meaningless*? Or is the word *"perceived"* implied by Rohr – *perceived* meaninglessness? In other words, is he suggesting that, even when life is purposeless from our human perspective, a higher purpose exists, unseen to us, from God's timeless viewpoint?

Finally, I got it.

---

[62] Richard Rohr, *Eager to Love* (London: Hodder & Stoughton, 2014), 72.

Life may at times seem absurd, as experienced by GOGs like Dave, or by people struggling to come to terms with life's apparently arbitrary tragedies and confusion. Faith is *not* trusting that there is *always, necessarily,* a higher purpose unknown to us. Faith is trusting God enough to accept this (*perceived or actual*) meaninglessness, *whether or not* there is a greater, unseen meaning to events!

Ultimately it comes down to a certain *experiential knowing* of the God of the cross, rather than knowing neat answers.

Christians like Dave and me believe that Jesus, by becoming a servant who washes feet, an innocent saviour who dies the crass death of the cruellest criminal, turned the world upside-down – or, rather, turns it back round the right way.

Through our cross-shaped faith, we see rights being ultimately wronged, the marginalised honoured, the arrogant brought down a peg or ten – and the absurdity of life becomes acceptable.

The cross gives faith-filled eyes a glimpse into a world beyond the one we see, where love is stronger than death and eternity is shaped by mercy.

The refreshingly down-to-earth founder of Care for the Family, Rob Parsons, reflecting on the homeless birth of Jesus and his own Christmas encounter with a homeless couple in central London, reminds us of some of Jesus' parting words to his flailing disciples:

> "'Do not let your hearts be troubled...My Father's house has many rooms...I am going there to prepare a place for you.'"

Rob goes on to explain:

> "It is as if, at the lowest moment of their lives, he wants them to grasp the reality of that other world. At the end of their journey there will be a welcome: all will be well."[63]

Those of us with faith "see" with our inner spirit the hope that lies beyond this world and are driven by that hope to make it a reality in *this* world. Knowing that "There are no homeless there, for everyone that's there has a home", as songwriter Kevin Prosch described heaven in *All I Need*[64], inspires us to mirror that vision this side of heaven. To bring the kingdom of heaven closer.

Or, in the words of the Christian Aid strapline: "We believe in life before death".

I think that, despite Dave's existential...*quandary*, shall we say (a problem allayed by croissants is no existential crisis!), he has some degree of subconscious acceptance of meaninglessness that shines through his evident peace, contentment and enjoyment of breakfast!

That subsurface understanding, now fortified by the *Eager to Love* dialogue, is traceable to his soul-deep trust in Christ and peace with God. Dave's endless motivation to serve people in need is a sign of his experience of knowing the God of the cross, a paradoxical outworking of his grace-full acceptance of life's absurdity.

***

I asked Dave the GOG what he thinks is *supposed* to be the ultimate meaning of life for Christians. His initial, off-the-cuff reply was: "To glorify God, I guess."

Fair enough, of course, for a Christian response.

But I bristle slightly at the kind of religious ideal of glorifying God – the kind of nebulous and potentially "radical" (in the wrong sense) idea that

---

[63] Rob Parsons. Beds for all who come. *Christianity* magazine. Dec 2016.
[64] Kevin Prosch, *All I Need*, from the album *Reckless Mercy*, Integrity Media, 1998.

gives rise to incorrigible idealism. The idea that "We must be right because we're doing this for the glory of God."

On the other hand, one of the top priorities in Jesus' prayer ("Hallowed be your name") *is* to see God being glorified, i.e. his character and presence being revealed to people everywhere. So maybe they (and Dave) are right in their aim, but I feel the need for a proviso...

....that glorifying God is like success or happiness: that it happens not by searching for it directly, but by setting our focus elsewhere.

They say that happiness and success are often found incidentally, by pursuing something else, like a creative or humanitarian cause, as Viktor Frankl wisely expressed like this:

> "Don't aim at success. The more you aim at it and make it a target, the more you are going to miss it. For success, like happiness, cannot be pursued; it must ensue, and it only does so as the unintended side effect of one's personal dedication to a cause greater than oneself or as the by-product of one's surrender to a person other than oneself." [65]

Maybe glorifying God is like that. Certainly the (fictitious but typical) people in Jesus' parable of the sheep and goats[66] weren't trying to be religious or glorify God. They were simply living out an instinctive heart of love, and in doing so were inadvertently serving Christ and glorifying God. How wonderful is that!

In the same way, as hinted earlier, humanitarian atheists might accidentally glorify God.

---

[65] Viktor Frankl, *Man's Search for Meaning* (London: Rider, 2004).
[66] Matthew 25:31-46

I was never a huge fan of those 80s songsters Frankie Goes to Hollywood – hence the aforementioned T-shirt! – but they did hit the nail right on the head when they acclaimed the power of love with these 4 golden words at Christmas 1984:

> Make love your goal.[67]

Singer/songwriter Holly Johnson once expressed ambitious aims for the song:

> "I always felt like The Power of Love was the record that would save me in this life. There is a Biblical aspect to its spirituality and passion; the fact that love is the only thing that matters in the end."

Pop stars can be surprisingly profound.

Earlier on, I described how John Lydon had turned out to be a misunderstood dark horse of integrity back in the old days of punk. In more recent years Lydon, now a less misunderstood, more respectable darling of middle-aged ex-punks, surprised half the world by asserting in an interview, "We just need to bloody love each other!" Johnny Rotten still knows what he's talking about.

Love surely has to be the ultimate meaning for every Christian. I think that, after some thought, Dave the GOG might agree with this.

Love, or relationship, is of course at the heart of the Christian faith:

> The Trinity marked by cords of intertwining love between Father, Son and Holy Spirit,

---

[67] Frankie Goes To Hollywood, The Power of Love, ZTT, 1984

extending out to humanity, culminating at the cross;

ordinary humans discovering the relief of being welcomed into the Father's arms,

being called into community with each other;

empowered to love the unlovable, and to forgive

even their enemies;

and, of almost greatest importance, those who truly believe this message of love find healing from their own self-disconnectedness, as they're able to do the hardest thing of all: forgive themselves.

Out of that restored relationship with self flows the strength to love others with the Father's love.

Even though I can be so task-oriented and goal-driven like a typical bloke, even sometimes avoiding people (just because I often feel the need to be alone), I believe that some of man's most significant meaning is found in personal relationship – in human connectedness.

It's one thing – and a necessary thing – to sign an online petition to house the homeless. It's far more *meaningful* to forge human contact with a homeless person and start to understand the man behind the sleeping-bag.

It's one thing – and a noble thing – to give money to charity to feed the hungry. It's far nobler, more God-like, to *get to know* a hungry person and to eat with her.

It's one thing – and a rare sign of community life – to help a neighbour move a sofa. It's far more satisfying and meaningful to engage in dialogue with that neighbour about his life (or yours) while moving that sofa.

I read on Facebook about an extraordinarily ordinary encounter between a young homeless man begging on the streets and a passer-by – except that the passer-by didn't pass by. He apologised for having no money to give, but spent time talking and listening.

The homeless man responded in this way:

> "It's not just about money lad, you've sat here and spoke to me, let me cry and vent, tell ya me story, know what I mean bro?! You've given me human contact and sometimes, after being ignored by thousands of people, that's all it takes lad."

Pure altruism is rare. Some would question its very existence. One of my homeless service colleagues, also a nurse, shamelessly confesses that she does her job to meet her own needs. I appreciate her model of honesty. We could tie ourselves up in knots questioning our motives – and never achieve anything in the process.

There have been times in writing this book when I've fretted over my narcissism, but the book still has to be written, for all sorts of good reasons, in spite of its elements of egocentricity – including this sentence! My "altruism" that I've spoken of is by no means pure selflessness, and I have no problem with that.

I know that when I make genuine human contact (I mean, the kind that involves some degree of mutual understanding, of *knowing* each other) with a homeless client or *any* human being – there is real meaningfulness for both *them* and *me*. A soul to soul connection.

Brian Thorne, the counsellor, made this astounding observation on his experience of deep human connection:

> "It seems as if for a space, however brief, two human beings are fully alive, because they have given themselves and each other

permission to risk being fully alive. At such a moment, I have no hesitation in saying that my client and I are caught up in a stream of love...

It sometimes seems that I receive my client whole and thereafter possess a knowledge of him or her which does not depend on biographical data. This understanding is intensely personal and invariably it affects the self-perception of the client and can lead to marked changes in attitude and behaviour. For me as a counsellor, it is accompanied by a sense of joy which, when I have checked it out, has always been shared by the client."[68]

Although within my work, the homeless and vulnerably housed individuals are by definition the focus of attention, I'm as valuable as – no more or less than – the next person, and I'm more than happy to share in the mutual benefits of humanitarianism. In the work that I do, it's win-win for clients and workers.

Some of the volunteers I've managed have told me they get far more out of volunteering than they put in.

Each of us benefits from knowing that we've connected. We're designed to gain happiness by making others happy.

As I mentioned before, the theory goes that the root cause of addiction, the common denominator, is disconnection: people feeling disconnected from family, society, themselves, and (some would add) God – often as a result of deep trauma or abuse.

---

[68] Brian Thorne, *Person-Centred Counselling: Therapeutic and spiritual dimensions* (London: Whurr), 77.

The more disconnected we are, the more likely we are to form tenacious bonds to things, substances or habits.

In services like the one I work for, fostering genuine, warm, human connections between addicted people and ourselves or others can be literally healing – one of the main ingredients in the recipe for recovery.

Within those connections, those "being with"s, meaning is not just in the giving, receiving, doing something for someone, or even in the verbal communication, but at the deeper level of restful existence with the other person, with ourselves, and with God.

At the heart of Christianity is *being*, starting way back with God, revealing his identity to Moses as *I Am* (or Yahweh).

Because God is the Source of all *being*, it's no surprise that he promises rest – a richness of existence – to those who come to him.

This is another of those truths that I'm still growing into...

***

But this entire chapter so far is really all a kind of preamble to describing the incredible sense of fulfilment that I'm so blessed to experience in my work.

Like many health and social care professionals, I was taught early on about Maslow's Hierarchy of Needs. Like many other professionals, I suspect, I never realised that the familiar triangular diagram was not actually formed by Maslow, nor that he intended far more flexibility for his model than it's normally given credit for.

Nevertheless, I've often considered how lucky I am to have tasted so (*unusually,* I think) richly of Maslow's ideal of self-actualisation.

The burning, yearning drive, planted in my soul during that unfathomable U-turn of autumn '87, to put the gifts I'd been given to useful service, has more than unfurled into job satisfaction; it's transpired into a fuller realisation of my identity and potential – who God made me to be and what he called me to do – for which I consider myself extraordinarily fortunate.

To quote neurologist and psychiatrist Viktor Frankl again, who knew a thing or two about this stuff:

> "The more one forgets himself – by giving himself to a cause to serve or another person to love – the more human he is and the more he actualizes himself. What is called self-actualization is not an attainable aim at all, for the simple reason that the more one would strive for it, the more he would miss it. In other words, self-actualization is possible only as a side-effect of self-transcendence."[69]

Frankl's view certainly makes sense of my own experience of self-actualisation growing out of my career choice – which I can't even say was entirely my own deliberate choice, but something I just *had* to pursue in response to God's branding of purpose on to my innermost soul.

***

And so, a few months after returning to the UK, living in Lewes, attending church and working out my future, I made the move to Brighton to work as an auxiliary in a nursing home to "try out" nursing before applying to train as an RGN.

Over about 18 months of care work across a few homes in Brighton & Hove, I witnessed some of the best and worst examples of care of the elderly. Even as a still very immature young man in my early 20s, by the

---

[69] Viktor Frankl, *Man's Search for Meaning* (London: Rider, 2004).

time I started my training in '89 I'd grown enough to want to make a difference to the world of care that I'd seen.

I was in one of the last cohorts to train as employees of the health authorities, before all nurse education was transferred out to the universities for better and/or worse.

In 1988 I was offered interviews at Worthing, Brighton and Eastbourne hospitals.

I didn't show up for the Brighton interview.

The landlord of the house I was sharing had given me a free pass to a fast food fair at Brighton Centre on the same day. Having already been accepted by Worthing, an interview with Brighton seemed quite unnecessary, and the idea of free food won the day! Some in my family would say that's the sign of a true Nuttall.

Later on, Worthing informed me they'd made the decision to change to Project 2000, meaning their students would no longer be paid employees of the health authority. I could see no way of supporting myself on a university course. Which meant my plan to train as a nurse now hung entirely on my interview at Eastbourne.

In view of my previous itinerant lifestyle, one of the interviewing tutors at Eastbourne District General Hospital wasn't convinced I was ready to settle into a 3-year commitment and advised me to return a year later if I was still interested. I was gutted – not only because I felt ready to start training there and then, but because this woman, judging me on the basis of my past rather than my present or aspired-to future, had failed to understand the massive internal change I'd undergone.

Couldn't she see that the old had gone and the new had come!

As someone who now interviews staff and volunteers, I hope I'm better than she was at giving prospective colleagues the benefit of the doubt, at discerning potential and promoting opportunities.

Nevertheless, I was undeterred and able to trust God, knowing that my times are in his hands. In retrospect, I was given another year to grow in character and gain experience as an auxiliary before embarking on the RGN course.

A year later I returned as advised to Eastbourne DGH, for a second interview. The same formidable tutor was there. The interview was touch-and-go.

I was called back into the interview room where, despite the resilience I'd displayed by coming back after a whole year, the tutor told me I lacked assertiveness and was going to reject me a second time.

I must admit, I'd found it hard to be assertive before this daunting woman who held my future in her hands. But I couldn't say that.

The other interviewing tutor was John, a man of unassuming confidence and a leader and first aid trainer with the organisation I work for now, a man committed to care. John seemed to see the potential, the genuine me who was more than ready to undertake this career. He wanted to give me a chance and was able to persuade his colleague to accept me for nurse training.

Phew!

And so, in Sept 1989, I embarked on the RGN course; I've never looked back.

Fifteen years later, I started my current employment, crossing paths with John once more. I made sure to thank him again for letting me in on the career that I love.

In the early '90s, as a newly qualified staff nurse, an elderly female patient I'd been looking after on a post-surgical ward commented to me with warmth in her eyes, "You're a born nurse."

As Van the Man might have said, that was a Wonderful Remark.

That kind of affirmation has been music to the ears of this person who was very nearly rejected from ever being given the chance to be what I was born to be.

***

One of the last things I did between leaving my job as an auxiliary in Hove and moving to Eastbourne to start my training was to take a trip to Amsterdam to sample their coffee bars and bring back a personal stash of hash and weed. Old habits die hard.

My relationship with cannabis, as mentioned earlier, was ambivalent for the first two years of my Christian life. As a young Christian who tended to think it was "wrong" (mainly because I saw it as a poor substitute for – and therefore barrier to – the experience of God's love), getting stoned was an area of intense psychological addiction, and I still felt the need for a smoke as an aid to relaxation.

Sometimes, as explored earlier in this chapter, meaning and purpose in events may be hard or impossible to understand. Other times, things make perfect sense in hindsight.

In the autumn of '89, a month or so into my nurse training, an experience of the Holy Spirit, again on my own in my room (but following prayer and a prophetic message for me in a church healing meeting), unlocked the ambivalence.

The cannabis use and my half-hearted approach to following Christ gave way to an overwhelming love for God, a renewed sense of his reality, and a new level of prayer and praise that flowed right from the heart. I felt the power of being forgiven in a way I hadn't done before – accompanied by tears and laughter in waves of God's accepting love.

It was one of the most intense, emotional, beautiful and liberating experiences of my life.

Cravings for cannabis were dissolved forever.

Later on, I realised it had been two years to the month (perhaps to the day, for all I know) since I had prayed "Well, God, I think I believe in you. I'm going to give this Christianity thing a try for a year or two and see what happens!"

I'd "tried" Christianity for two years, and as a result found a permanent home in God's heart. The book says, "Taste and see..." I'd tasted of this new life; it tasted good, it had taken hold of me, and I never needed to taste cannabis ever again.

It seems that God might take us at our word, so be careful what you pray for!

***

During my 5 years in Eastbourne – 3 years training followed by 2 years as a staff nurse on a ward at the DGH – I became religiously zealous, largely through the influence of the kind of church I'd joined, although it was also an authentic response to the new life I was still discovering. Reaching out to others to tell them about Jesus became a bit of an obsession, as I liberally dished out leaflets advertising church events and personal tracts that summarised my story of faith, or went on to the streets to speak to young people about Jesus.

So consumed was I with all things church throughout the 90s, that a whole world of popular culture passed me by. My oldest son, Jonathan, who's a bit of a music buff, was horrified to learn that I knew virtually nothing about Britpop or grunge. Yes, I was vaguely aware of Oasis and Nirvana, but that was about the sum of it. In more recent years I've discovered and fallen in love with the sounds of Chris Cornell with Soundgarden and, later, Audioslave. I was honestly, deeply shocked and saddened by Cornell's sudden death this year.

On one occasion in the early '90s I was rightly reprimanded by a ward sister for "preaching" to a patient. I got up the noses of plenty of colleagues and I'm sure I put a few people off Jesus and Christianity forever. I was the religious version of a reformed smoker – only worse! It wasn't *all* bad, though. I was sincere, I tried to back up my beliefs with genuine care for people, and closer colleagues tended to respect my faith. A few even saw through the Bible-bashing exterior to the positive reality behind it and found a new or renewed faith of their own.

I'd sometimes be asked by these colleagues who saw my zeal whether I was considering becoming a priest or vicar. The truth is that, despite such fervour, church leadership never held any appeal. At the same time I was itching to take a break from nursing to work full-time in some kind of Christian outreach, and so I applied for a Frontier Year Project.

This voluntary training / outreach programme with the New Frontiers group of churches was partially tailored to the individual applicant, and so in September 1994 I was offered a place in South East London with South Lee Christian Church which – together with Hither Green Baptist Church – was setting up a homeless outreach project.

It was through this partnership that I was involved in visiting Ennersdale House (formerly Spur House), the large local hostel, and setting up the

Saturday morning drop-in centre at HGBC, where we met beautiful people like 28p Jonny.

I treasured working within this inter-church collaboration: a love for Christ and compassion for the poor that crossed denominational boundaries – the sort of unity that seems to attract heaven's seal of approval.

One particular highlight was praying for a middle-aged homeless man named Bob. Whenever we sat and prayed with him, he'd drop on to the church hall carpet, stay there in a state of bliss for a minute or two, his lined face wrapped in a big, wide smile, and eventually get up describing the experience as like having taken "a massive Valium tablet"! It was such a delight to see someone in dire circumstances of life being moved by heaven's joy.

There were many people from those "drop-in days" who hold a special place in my heart. Not just the homeless people: also volunteers like Mark & Diana, Bill & Kath, Liz, Alistair and others, who journeyed with me for those few years in a learning curve about faith, homelessness and ourselves.

There's one person in particular who deserves a special mention: Rev Richard Blyth, minister of Hither Green Baptist Church, a man with a humble heart as big as an ocean and enough uniqueness to be on a level with people like me and our homeless friends.

It was the early days of Alpha, the inter-denominationally popular course that helps people explore Christianity. Richard had decided to run the course at HGBC on a series of Sunday mornings. Each session starts with a talk, followed by open discussion in small groups, which in this case included a bespoke group for the homeless men from Ennersdale House who'd been coming to the church.

I (from South Lee Christian Church) had been tasked by Richard with leading this group, with support from Janine (from HGBC), who went on to volunteer at the drop-in. And that's how the two of us met!

We love Richard, who catalysed our introduction, married us and counselled us. He and his wife Rachel remain our good friends to this day.

London became my home for 10 years. Janine and I started our family, and I returned to nursing while continuing the homeless support and outreach. Friends moved away, life took over, the drop-in eventually came to an end, and in 2004 we moved to Hastings.

I'm so blessed to have a marriage that from the start was grounded in shared purpose and values.

***

Absence of purpose is a problem of life, according to philosophers. I guess many people in our disconnected and consumerist culture struggle to identify real purpose to their lives, aside from the urge to pass on one's genes to the next generation.

For me, fulfilment has flourished in the shape of my work, as I've had the incredibly good fortune to be able to put to outward, practical expression all the passions, abilities and spiritual qualities that God has rooted deep within me. It's hard to express the fullness of that feeling.

US author Frederick Buechner defined vocation as "where your deepest gladness meets the world's deepest need". I think I know something of that happy meeting-place, which is a kind of home.

Growing into one's vocation is one sort of homecoming, as my favourite eccentric, Vincent van Gogh, realised. In a letter to his brother Theo, he wrote this about his own vocation:

"I mean, painting is a *home*..." (emphasis mine).

However, I also know full well, from my own experience of living out-of-kilter, the dangers of finding our ultimate meaning in what we do: the risk of losing identity apart from our work; the risk of workaholism and burn-out; of depression when we're made redundant or take retirement; the threats posed to marriages and family relationships; and the paramount importance of discovering deepest meaning in *being*.

Despite (or perhaps prompted by) this blessing of self-actualisation, I've increasingly re-discovered the child-like need to continually return to the Source of this life that I've been given and to nurture the identity I've been given in the Father's love.

Brennan Manning, that masterful conveyor of compassion, expressed it like this:

> "While the impostor draws his identity from past achievements and the adulation of others, the true self claims identity in its belovedness. We encounter God in the ordinariness of life: not in the search for spiritual highs and extraordinary, mystical experiences but in our simple presence in life."[70]

For me, contemplative prayer and mindful rest have been essential keys to this personal (re-)development.

Those too immersed in their work or projects risk developing a false or superficial persona, in the same way as anyone who has experienced drug addiction.

I've heard a few individuals I've worked with, who were caught in the vice-like grip of crack and heroin use, wail with tears of desperate anguish, "I just want to be me again!" Addictions rob us of our identity.

[70] Brennan Manning, *Abba's Child: The Cry of the Heart for Intimate Belonging* (Colorado Springs: Navpress, 2015).

We all derive a certain sense of self-knowledge from our attachments: whether activities, loved ones or possessions. Our homes and projects and *stuff of life* tend to be a projection of who we are – our passions, personalities and potential. They help to reinforce and remind us of who we are and who we want to be. That's not a bad thing.

But it's another reason why homeless people are especially prone to depression. Without a place of their own to express and reflect their personality and aspirations, a sense of identity is often eroded away. This, together with the huge losses (not only of homes and relationships, but often also jobs, opportunities and more), is a recipe for major depression, anxiety, substance misuse, addiction, and suicide. One study put the rate of suicide amongst rough sleepers as 35 times that of the general population.

Provision of housing tends to be the first step that needs to be taken before other needs can be effectively tackled. As I read in a quote by an ex-homeless person in an exhibition about housing in Weston Park Museum in Sheffield,

> "If you don't have a base, even if it's a bad base, you can't come to terms with who you are, right now."

However, at the risk of stating the obvious, the solution to homelessness is usually more than bricks and mortar and as complex and individual as the needs of the person concerned.

No surprise, then, that governments and statutory agencies, with the best will in the world and the aid of voluntary organisations, struggle so hard to provide adequate solutions.

Unfortunately, under current Conservative government, politicians don't even seem to demonstrate much good will, and the unnecessary rise in homelessness continues relentlessly.

Working in one of those voluntary organisations, in partnership with many other like-minded colleagues in a range of agencies, together doing our best to support homeless people towards housing, health and well-being, is an enormous privilege. I like to try and nurture these individuals' own sense of identity, meaning and purpose, in the hope of helping to unlock their ability to engage with the recovery process.

In doing so, there is a twofold blessing:

I progress on my own pilgrimage home to self-actualisation;

And a potential homecoming to meaning and self-realisation awaits those homeless individuals just as it did for me.

17: Blessed are the sandwich-dunkers

(coming home to me)

> *The curious paradox is that when I accept myself just as I am, then I can change.*
> Carl Rogers

"You've found yourself," suggested my friend, Millie, when I attempted to explain my conversion in those early days of faith.

"No, I found Jesus," I retorted smugly with the knowing smile of newfound religion.

I cringe at some of the things I said 30 years ago, 10 years ago...or even yesterday. And I try to be easy on myself.

No doubt, in 30 years time if I'm still alive, or even tomorrow, I'll be cringing at some of the things I've said today. If we're self-aware and intent on personal growth, we change and mature and tend to prefer the person we are to the person we were, while longing for something better still.

When I recall stupid things people have said to me in the past, I try to remember my own faux pas and to be as forgiving to them as I need them to be towards me.

It took me a very short time to realise that Millie and I were *both* right, and if we'd had that conversation today, I'd acknowledge that fact and enjoy our common ground. Neither of our statements was in fact stupid, but they were only half true, and together they formed a greater, 3-D truth.

Of course I'd found myself. And it was *also of course* because I'd found Jesus, or he'd found me, however cheesy that may sound: the whole discovery of purpose, that I'm so fortunate to have been given, this unfolding of my identity, that I'm still enjoying, founded on faith.

I'm sure this is blindingly obvious by this point in the book, but although I'd found a spiritual home in God, it was *equally* a homecoming to *me*. However, this person who found a home in his own skin is still, like everyone else, broken and dysfunctional in parts. What makes this brokenness bearable (for me) is learning to live in the divine beauty and mystery of splintered humanity.

Christians pray for healing. Some of us *work* for healing. Therapists, counsellors, priests, spiritual directors, friends, and even medical professionals like me can be agents for change. I pursue realisation of the potential for wholeness of soul, mind and spirit for myself and others. But there is also serenity in the acceptance of imperfection. Serenity rooted in *wild, unbridled trust* in God's reckless love. Sometimes I just need to say, *this is me* and "me" is OK.

Brennan Manning, once again, has helped me absorb this truth, illustrated by the following quotes:

> "If you love yourself intensely and freely, then your feelings about yourself correspond perfectly to the sentiments of Jesus... Acceptance is absolute, without inquiry into the past, without special conditions, so that the liberated sinner can live again, accept himself, forgive himself, love himself."[71]

---

[71] Brennan Manning, *Reflections for Ragamuffins* (New York: HarperOne, 1998), 163, 48.

"Before I am asked to show compassion toward my brothers and sisters in their suffering, He asks me to accept His compassion in my own life, to be transformed by it, to become caring and compassionate toward myself in my own suffering and sinfulness, in my own hurt, failure and need."[72]

Home is a resting place in this broken soul, contentment in the "now and not yet" of our own faltering humanity within the broad sweep of the Father's eternal viewpoint.

* * *

Meanwhile, on TV...

The argument escalated between the two friends until the detective slung a stinging, intensely personal accusation against the priest, which the refreshingly human priest, Sidney, understood as it was intended: a sordid slur on his character.

"Why do you always side with the bad guys?" shouted Geordie, the cop. "I know why! IT'S BECAUSE YOU SEE YOURSELF IN THEM, ISN'T IT?!"

The insult resulted in a bloody nose inflicted by the unorthodox vicar on his detective friend.

As I watched the scene unfold in the second series of the ITV drama, *Grantchester*, I was taken aback by Sidney's reaction at being told he sees himself in the bad guys. I was genuinely anticipating him interpreting the reproach positively.

If it were me, I'd have taken it as a *compliment* on my ability to identify with the disenfranchised!

---

[72] Brennan Manning, *The Relentless Tenderness of Jesus* (Grand Rapids: Revell, 2005).

Not long ago, I had a eureka moment. It dawned on me that one of the reasons I feel such affinity with the people I work with is *not just* because I *was* messed-up and lost and homeless and then my life turned around; it's just as much because I'm so aware of the struggles and weaknesses I *still* face.

I don't find it difficult to "side with the bad guys". The ex-offenders; the ones who disengage, who break the rules and generally mess things up for themselves. I see a bit of them in me.

King David (who messed up just a bit) says in the Psalms that "even darkness is as light" to God. I'm learning that what we think of as spiritual or psychological darkness (our own or others') may well be where we find God, and that our faults and brokenness might be just as valuable tools as our perceived strengths and abilities.

Manning, describing the experiences of Catherine of Siena, says that

> "She had lost the presence of God, only to find it again in the deep darkness of a richer faith. She had learned to celebrate the darkness."[73]

Carl Jung coined the wonderful term "wounded healer", claiming that

> "a good half of every treatment that probes at all deeply consists in the doctor's examining himself... it is his own hurt that gives a measure of his power to heal."[74]

Jung's closest colleague, Marie Louise Franz, went as far as saying that

> "the wounded healer IS the archetype of the Self and is at the bottom of all genuine healing procedures."[75]

---

[73] Brennan Manning, *Reflections for Ragamuffins* (New York: HarperOne, 1998), 82.

[74] Anthony Stevens, *Jung* (Oxford: OUP, 1994), 110.

[75] Wikipedia: Wounded Healer. https://en.wikipedia.org/wiki/Wounded_healer

Or, as Yalom put it,

> "Perhaps wounded healers are effective because they are more able to empathize with the wounds of the patient; perhaps it is because they participate more deeply and personally in the healing process."[76]

I find it immensely reassuring that my own experience confirms this idea. I'm certain that my woundedness, as much as my clinical skills, informs my professional capability. I relate to therapist Jan Hawkins, who found that:

> "The day I realised I would never be 'cured' was very liberating, and I now prefer to think in terms of the wounded healer. Acknowledging my own woundedness...has allowed me to come closer to my own clients in their suffering." [77]

***

One part of my baggage, that I've struggled to come to terms with, is a tendency to compare myself unfavourably with others, instead of seeing myself as a unique, equally valuable (id)entity.

While "finding myself" has entailed amazing change and personal growth, age and maturity have taught me that self-discovery also means embracing those less desirable, darker places of my heart, that to God are light and as fully accepted as the nicer bits of me.

And that, paradoxically, the change we still desire, as Rogers suggested in the quote above, is more likely to come through self-acceptance.

---

[76] Irvin Yalom, *The Gift of Therapy* (London: Piatkus, 2002), 109.

[77] Jan Hawkins, in a chapter entitled: Walking the Talk: Potent therapy is a risky business. In Jeff Leonardi (ed.), *The human being fully alive* (Ross-on-Wye: PCCS, 2010), 26.

An obvious example of this is anxiety. Charlie Brown, in *Peanuts*, lamented that even his anxieties have anxieties! It's a common problem – to feel anxious about being anxious. But when we accept that it's normal and OK to feel anxious, the original anxiety has less power over us and tends to reduce.

As a younger Christian, I used to compare myself with church friends, evoking feelings of inadequacy. I wasn't as zealous, as faithful, as pure, as certain of my faith, as... (fill in the adjective).

According to a brief video I saw online, "Most of our insecurities come from comparing our behind-the-scenes with other people's highlight reels." Well put. There is much truth in pop psychology, and this principle applies to life in general, not just to social media.

I still fall into the comparison trap – it's a hard habit to break. Self-compassion is a lesson I'm still learning.

But in my formative years as a young Christian, I learned an important lesson. One that I've held on to, and that involved (among others things) a dream and a sandwich-dunking incident.

So there we were, some good friends from the church, enjoying a cuppa and some snacks in the Wish Tower Cafe in Eastbourne. You'll remember, I'd moved to the sunny, conservative town in '89 to train as a nurse, and here I became an integral part of a thriving, evangelical church.

I was still quite new to this Christianity lark, this was my first period of real church commitment, and I was keen to learn what it meant to live this new life.

As I'd done a thousand times before (well, quite a few times, at least), I dunked my cheese sandwich into my coffee in front of these friends, as we nattered about life and stuff. Nothing wrong with that – coffee and cheese sandwich make a great combination. You should try it.

My friend Chris, who was an evangelist and a sort of leader in the church, commented on the sandwich-dunking. Not unkindly, just light-heartedly teaching me in a mentor-y sort of way some decorum. Apparently it wasn't the thing to do.

"Don't you know the 11th Evangelical Commandment?" he asked, tongue quite firmly in a smiling cheek: "Thou shalt conform!"

It was a mixed message. On the one hand, he was implying the absurdity of an unwritten church code of conformity; on the other, he was subliminally reinforcing that absurd rule by teaching me a certain brand of social ethics.

I've often thought about that brief conversation and reflected on the unspoken pressure within churches – or *any* organisation – to conform; and my own self-imposed pressure to live up to the ideals of some other person's qualities *as I (in a usually twisted, false kind of way) perceive them.*

Churches can unwittingly – or intentionally, in some cases – enforce adherence to a single set of values, behaviours and beliefs, even on peripheral and controversial issues, failing to allow for different personalities and life experiences to shape the way we perceive life and faith and the way we relate to God.

"Believe and behave exactly like us, or you don't really belong" is the vibe we might feel is being communicated.

Conformity is an insidious hazard. Not only do we risk losing our identity, but for Christians, we deprive churches – deprive *Jesus* – of a precious individual part of his body. The church – again, *any* organisation – is made a poorer place when its people don't feel able to be true to themselves. The church needs its poets, its artists, its hippies, its misfits, and even its "heretics". These are often the prophets who challenge the status quo and help shape the church into a people that reflect the welcoming, home-making heart of Jesus.

It needs its activists, its eccentrics, kooks and cranks, its schizophrenics, and its advocates of liberal thinking.

It needs its sarnie-dunkers.

Around that time, though, when I wasn't busy making detrimental comparisons that denied who I was, or taking lessons in social graces, I instinctively befriended people sleeping in the shelters on Eastbourne seafront and got alongside others I met who had mental health problems. I brought them to church and supported them in any way I could.

I started volunteering with EAH – Eastbourne Action for the Homeless (a project which unfortunately folded a couple of years later).

I've already mentioned Steven, who was befriended by some District General Hospital friends and me, but who sadly died there in the shelter by the sea. There was another man in that shelter with him: Graham, an older, northern man with a painful limp and a walking stick, who (like Steven) struggled to get about. I knew nothing about the housing system then, or whether he'd have been eligible for any help from the Council, but I suspect not.

He readily accepted our friendship and help. My friends Clare, Sue and Carolyn, midwives who shared one of the DGH residences and, like me, were part of ACTS, the hospital Christian Union, broke the accommodation rules and took some risks, letting Graham sleep on their floor for a few nights.

As Gandhi's and King's lives taught us, no one ever won battles against social injustice by sticking to rules.

We didn't even really know Graham's story – how he'd ended up homeless. Perhaps we didn't think to ask, or maybe we just took him at face value and allowed him to tell us what he wanted in his own time. Graham did tell us that he'd loved somebody once – they had been engaged – but the girl had been murdered. He said he couldn't forgive her murderer. You couldn't help but sympathise with Graham.

You could tell a part of him was locked up, locked in, by these inevitable, tormented feelings of loss and anger and resentment. The bereavement was his nadir, the moment that set the course of his life on a new trajectory.

My guess is that the resultant anger, depression, or feelings of being unable to cope, were in some way behind his loss of accommodation. A typical chain reaction of losses, culminating in homelessness and hopelessness, that needed help from outside – or above – to break.

We took him to church. He even came to ACTS. We taught him about the two-way forgiveness found in Christ. The inseparable double act of forgiving and being forgiven. He cried when he took communion; there was meaning for him in remembering Christ's suffering.

We found him a place to live – his own room in shared, supported housing, owned and run by Lyn, a nurse and all-round amazing person, who I'd got to know through another friend she'd accommodated. Graham found faith in Christ, and forgiveness. They say that when you forgive, you set the captive free and that the captive is *you*. This was never truer than in Graham's case. He couldn't change his own or his fiancée's past, but he was able, with God's help, to change his future. He settled into the house, bought a budgie, and lived there happily for many years until his death. I have a touching, black-and-white photo I took of Graham's smiling face, content in his new surroundings, peering through the bars of the birdcage, making cooing noises at the budgie – the bird the only one of the two now caged.

Long after I'd moved on from Eastbourne, I was informed that Graham had passed away. I heard that he'd been grateful to the end towards those who had helped him, that he'd lived and died at peace with God and himself.

***

It was during that period of finding my feet on the streets, "being with" homeless people, that Chris, he of sandwich etiquette fame, complimented me on the way I was able to get alongside people who were, in his words, "a bit odd".

Maybe not quite how I would have phrased it!

But I could see it was true, even if I couldn't understand why the whole church wasn't doing something so obviously Christian as helping the homeless and reaching those on the margins rather than simply proliferating a middle-class model.

I was still discovering the uniqueness of my calling and purpose, not only to support homeless people, but also to remind my own little corner of the late 20th Century church of its practical mission, the "social gospel" that some had regarded as almost irrelevant in its quest to save souls.

Thankfully, today's UK church, more widely now than then, accepts the obvious belief that God cares about whole people, not just body-less spirits.

***

Also around that time, I had a dream. Not one of Martin Luther King magnitude, but of significant influence and import to my own life journey. In my dream, I was in a kerbside gutter, tending to a homeless person, feeling very much at home in the situation. I turned to my good friend, Steve, to whom I'd always negatively compared myself, a "real" Christian, faithful and committed (not like me), and proclaimed to him with excited joy, "I've found my ministry!!"

The dream was massive in enabling me to start to see who I was and the unique place I had in the church. It didn't completely cure my inclination towards unhealthy comparisons, but it sure helped.

Like much of the metamorphosis I went through as a young Christian, supporting homeless people was not so much an act of obedience to the Bible or even Jesus (although there was that too), more a natural outworking of who I was.

To use John Ortberg's wonderfully expressive term, I was becoming more "you-ier"![78] I could hardly *not* do these things.

***

Coming home to me has not been all about supporting homeless people or about what I do, though; wrapped up in the discovery of my identity has been the emerging of a you-ier *spirituality* as well.

---

[78] John Ortberg, *The Me I Want To Be* (London: Zondervan, 2014).

Rewind to Halloween '87, and I'm hitching a ride to the Grand Canyon on one of my last USA experiences, before returning to the UK.

I'd stepped into faith just weeks earlier and had very little understanding of what that meant or what was in store, only that I'd changed at the deepest level and honestly believed in God.

I got into a conversation about faith with the guy who'd picked me up en route from Flagstaff, Arizona, to the canyon. He wasn't like the fundamentalist Christians I'd met previously, but he believed in Jesus. He spoke about the significance of the alignment of certain planets and other "new-agey" ideas – and yet the most important thing for him, the centre of all things, somehow was... Jesus.

The Grand Canyon beckoned me into its beautiful arms, my head swimming delightfully with these awesome thoughts about a grand Universe held together at every level by Christ.

This wasn't the first time on my travels I'd met someone who embraced broader ideas than those of mainstream Christianity but for whom Jesus was central. And each one left an indelible impression.

Months later, in the UK, a lady in the church I started attending asked me if there was a Bible verse that had been of particular significance in my conversion. My reply was John 14:6, in which Jesus makes the startling and at first sight exclusivist claim to be "the way, the truth and the life. No one comes to the Father but through me."

I'd become convinced of the reality of Jesus' claims about himself and – I confess – somewhat impressed by the apparent conviction, certainty even, expressed in the faith of many Christians I'd met along the road.

And yet, when I later reflected on this period, it took me a long time to grasp how I'd managed to have simultaneously embraced the apparently exclusive claims of Christianity and more pluralistic views of others.

In the ensuing years, I got swept up into the exclusivist ways that sometimes creep into evangelical church. Religion can have the unfortunate tendency to dictate who's in and who's out. The instinctive tribalism inherent in humanity.

To be fair, Jesus himself spoke of the way being narrow, and it sometimes seems hard to reconcile this kind of statement with his broader, inclusive teachings.

But I've learned since to understand all of Jesus' words in the context of his whole teaching and ministry – one of blatant bias towards the casualties of class systems and the victims of religion; the context of a kingdom that overturns social injustice.

If the way is narrow and some are left out, it's because the ruling rich and religious autocrats (amongst others) have excluded *themselves* and missed the way, through elitism, entitlement, and elevating themselves over "lesser mortals"[79]. The way is not missed by simply following the wrong belief system.

I no longer find it hard to understand how Jesus and pluralism co-exist much more happily than some might accept.

It seems clear that God's light and compassion are big enough to percolate through all our imperfect, diverse, human ideas about religion and spirituality to all those whose hearts are longing for the truth and love that are embodied in Jesus, *even if they don't call it "Jesus"*.

---

[79] As in *The Rich Man and Lazarus*, one of Jesus' parables, found in Luke 16.

Richard Rohr put it like this:

> "*Conversion, therefore, is not joining a different group, but seeing with the eyes of the crucified.* The cross is Paul's philosopher's stone or 'code breaker' for any lasting spiritual liberation. God can save sincere people of faith inside of any system or religion, if only they can be patient, trusting, and compassionate in the presence of human misery or failure, especially their own. This is life's essential journey. These trustful ones have surrendered to Christ, very often without needing to use the precise word 'Christ' at all (Matthew 7:21). It is the doing not the saying that matters."[80]

But this is not a theology book, except in the sense that it tells the story of my own, personal, spiritual journey. I make these points simply to illustrate the latter stages of my homecoming to me, in which I've discovered the breathtaking liberty of accepting my own outlook rather than attempting and failing to conform to someone else's pattern of faith. Dogmatism doesn't sit comfortably with me. I'm one of those people who say, "This is what I believe, *but I could be wrong.*"

On the one hand, I hold my convictions deeply, and like those Christians I met on the road, I can't help sharing my story with others, *because it really has been good news.*

On the other hand, I can't say to others, "You must believe what I believe," because somehow the truth seems too big for such singularity.

***

When I first ventured back on the road in '87, I knew I was searching for something and had this fanciful idea of sitting, meditating on a

---

[80] Richard Rohr, *Eager to Love* (London: Hodder & Stoughton, 2014).

mountaintop for years in that quest – while never actually expecting to find anything. As it happened, it was a surprising blend of experience and conversations more than a silent retreat into solitude that culminated in the unexpected answer that found *me*.

Most surprising of all was the role that human interaction played in the whole process – the acts of kindness, the conversations, debates and arguments with people of faith, the look of life in the eyes of Christians, the examples of integrity in people like Ray. And the enthusiasm and faith of these people who couldn't help but tell others their story of genuine transformation.

It was those moments of "being with", of human connecting, that ultimately sparked connection with God.

I can't ignore those memories, nor the call of Jesus to now forge those human connections with others myself and to tell my own story, as I'm doing here.

At the same time, I recognise the importance of being true to my introvert self, that's come full circle in that attraction to solitude and meditation. It's funny how things turn out.

Like so much of the spiritual life, it's a case of avoiding dualism in favour of both/and, rather than either/or. Human connection and solitude are equally important.

A more broad and contemplative approach to prayer and faith is where I'm at home. I can't say for certain, "This is the path that every person, or even every Christian, should take", nor am I promoting the contemplative path as a panacea for every spiritual ill; I can only say that this is where I belong, right now.

I can also say with 100% conviction, that if I were writing this book in 10 years' time, the spirituality and theology that I've described as an expression of who I am would take on a different flavour again, yet still (I hope) Christ-centred. Hence, I feel it's worth repeating that this is not a theology book, simply an account of my own subjective outlook, but one that I hope will be of some help to others.

The Bible encourages us to "Be still and know that I am God." In stillness before an unknowable God, yet paradoxically self-disclosed through Jesus, we discover a unique kind of knowing.

In contemplative prayer, we experience a certain sense of immersion into God and nature. The truths we believe, the love we claim, and the beauty we enjoy, surround us, soak us and remain with us. A heartfelt, Imax kind of knowing, rather than a cerebral, two-dimensional knowing.

Stillness fosters awe at the world and consciousness of God's inextricable presence in it. We're inclined to take ourselves, our partisan politics, divisive doctrines and intellectualism a little less seriously in the light of such knowing.

Silence before the infinite and ineffable instils in us the feeling of being part of something so much bigger than the things we know and believe.

An atheist friend of mine, Brian, told me, "Where I differ from you is that religious people feel the need to have answers, whereas I'm happy to live with mystery, *not* to have answers."

To which I replied, "Well, actually, we have that in common. I love mystery too, and any religious person who says they have all the answers clearly has a different idea of God than I do."

He seemed pleasantly surprised at our consensus. We also agreed on how beautiful it is to be able to re-capture, in middle age, that sense of wonder that most of us lose with our innocence in the transition from children into adulthood. Although Wordsworth opined,

> *"My heart leaps up when I behold*
>
> *a rainbow in the sky;*
>
> *So was it when my life began,*
>
> *So is it now I am a man,*
>
> *So be it when I shall grow old",*

...I think we rediscover wonder in a slightly different way as adults. We understand something of the science behind a rainbow – we know there's no pot of gold, but the hard facts don't detract from the wonder and the mystery; they may even enhance it.

Brian entered his "second age of wonder", as we might call it, after a near-death experience following a stroke. An ex-heroin and general drug addict, 20 years clean, Brian said that after the stroke he would look at a cloud and go "Wow!" with a new sense of awe. He sees the world around him with new eyes, wondrous at every stroke of nature, with every temptation back to drugs apparently gone forever.

Or as another atheist, the philosopher and author A.C. Grayling, has observed,

> *"If you really want a mind-altering experience, look at a tree."*

My reintroduction to wonder has been prompted largely by an intentionally more mindful approach to faith and life. But whatever the instigator, it was a joy to be able to share such solidarity with Brian, atheist and Christian together revelling in a universe beyond words.

As well as being one of my favourite eccentrics, Vincent van Gogh is one of my favourite *contemplatives* – a quality expressed not only in his magical depictions of fields and skies that move me to tears, but also in his writings. He put this in a letter to his brother Theo in 1882:

> "I see that nature has told me something, has spoken to me, and that I have to put it down in shorthand. In my shorthand there may be words that cannot be deciphered, there may be mistakes or gaps; but there is something of what that wood or beach or figure has told me in it, and it is not the tame or conventional language derived from a studied manner or a system, but rather that from nature itself."

And I…sometimes, when I stop…

and stop…

and stop…

and absorb the golden sights and smells

and sounds (and silence) of nature,

bathing in the Creator's brushstrokes, I find my soul re-awakened to his presence, and a smirk sometimes spreads across my face… a smile even, and occasionally a laugh springs up from those wells of the Spirit deep within, and I feel a little high in the Love that created these wonders around me, and my spirit is refreshed once again.

And now perhaps I understand something of what Van Morrison (my other favourite Van) meant when he wrote *And It Stoned Me*[81]. The song describes a time in Van's childhood when an everyday experience of drinking fresh water from a mountain stream near Ballystockart in Ireland took on an extraordinary, even mystical, quality, a bit like….being stoned.

---

[81] Van Morrison, *And It Stoned Me*, from the Album *Moondance*, Warner Bros, 1970.

How wonderful to recognise that experience as a 12-year-old child! It comes as no surprise, then, that Van Morrison expresses in so many of his songs a nostalgic yearning for the enchanting simplicity of the rural Irish life he remembers so fondly.

For many of us adults, that kind of experience develops when we willingly allow ourselves to be embraced, like children, by the Father's love, not striving to be religious or even spiritual perhaps, but being still, trusting and resting in I Am, who is Love.

The night before reaching the Grand Canyon in '87 I stayed in a travellers' hostel in Flagstaff, where I chatted with a seasoned hiker. You know the type – one of those smugly healthy types with all the gear: the boots, the proper camping equipment. Not like me in my T-shirt, trainers and shoulder bag containing a sleeping-bag. I didn't even have a rucksack at this point, after I'd lost it all overnight to some opportunist in those bushes.

"Fresh air's the only high I need," retorted the outdoor enthusiast, *smugly*, after I revealed that I liked getting stoned in picturesque, away-from-it-all places.

Well, that killed the conversation.

And although I wouldn't want to emulate his smugness, it does feel good to know that purer high that we were designed to enjoy without the aid of mind-altering substances.

***

A little while ago I met a beautiful, jolly Catholic, who shared my interest in meditative prayer and admiration for Thomas Merton, the popular 20th Century contemplative writer. This man informed me wickedly with a wry smile that Merton, a Catholic himself, had been responsible for converting more Catholics to Buddhism than anyone else!

It's probably not true. If it is, the irony is as delicious as a tub of Ben & Jerry's cookie dough ice cream. More likely, and probably better, is that Merton (perhaps unintentionally) fostered not so much conversion but *convergence*.

Although he extolled the benefits of contemplation from a distinctly Christian viewpoint, the parallels with Eastern or Buddhist meditation can hardly be lost on Merton's readers.

There are some religious people who recoil at the very thought of anything associated with another faith, clinging to their religion in fear that they may be negatively affected by an unhealthy spiritual influence. I can sympathise, as I was one of them.

But the person whose trust has developed from religion-centred to Jesus-centred becomes less worried by differences of faith and finds Christ in surprising places.

In contrast with my early – and probably necessary – choice between Buddhist ideas and Jesus, these days I identify with that driver in Arizona with his appealing syncretism, and smile with delight at the idea of a (Jesus-centred) convergence of faiths.

I'm reminded of a time a few years ago when I was at a training session with a colleague who I knew to be a Buddhist, but other than that we hardly knew each other and I'm sure he didn't know I was a Christian. After I'd said something about buying ethical goods, he told me with a grin, "You'd make a good Buddhist."

"Well, I hope I'd make a good Christian as well," was my inner response. "But what is a good Christian?" I then mused. "And in any case, is there such a thing as a good Christian?"

Wrestling with this internal dialogue, I was at a complete loss for words to actually *say* and all I could do was quietly accept the compliment, which was just the right thing to do.

If it sounds like I'm writing off more black-and-white expressions of Christianity – I'm not. I owe a huge deal to evangelical, even fundamentalist Christians – to the people who dared to share their faith with me in the hovels, hostels and highways of America, to the churches I joined as a younger Christian, and to my current church, Holy Trinity Hastings, which I love being part of. Although evangelical in theology (which really just means the leaders' approach to the Bible is probably a little tighter than mine), HTH is embracing of difference and outsiders. Where there is a sharing of orthopraxy and humility of heart, orthodoxy fades to the background.

These people have all positively shaped me in numerous ways.

It's just that I no longer find myself able to adhere to the mechanistic, rigid thinking and verbose worship expressions of faith that often characterise mainstream Christianity and make me feel just a little bit claustrophobic, without being untrue to myself and therefore to the God who made me.

The path to this place hasn't been easy. On the drive to authenticity, there have been conflicts with some who hold a stricter view of things; heartache and rejection for me and my family. It seems that Brennan Manning shared the exact same experience (forgive me for quoting him yet again):

"The poverty of uniqueness is the call of Jesus to stand utterly alone when the only alternative is to cut a deal at the price of one's integrity. It is a lonely *yes* to the whispers of our true self, a clinging to our core identity when companionship and community support are withheld. It is a courageous determination to make unpopular decisions that are expressive of the truth of who we are – not of who we think we should be or whom someone else wants us to be. It is trusting enough in Jesus to make mistakes and believing enough that his life will still pulse within us. It is the unarticulated, gut-wrenching yielding of our true self to the poverty of our own unique, mysterious personality."[82]

Despite the wounds sustained along the way, I wouldn't swap this place for anything. To stand in integrity is to bask in light. Which is where Jesus seems to be.

***

One aspect of this spiritual identity that's developed in me over the years has been voiced aptly by Richard Rohr, drawing on the Franciscan spirituality that's inspired his own monastic movement, The Center for Action and Contemplation.

He describes the early followers of St Francis as living life *on the edge of the inside*.

In any organisation there are some who serve at the core, where decisions are made. Then there are outsiders, who might be hostile towards – or simply have no interest in – the group.

---

[82] Brennan Manning, *Abba's Child: The Cry of the Heart for Intimate Belonging* (Colorado Springs: Navpress, 2015).

But the people in the third position – at the edge of the inside – are within the organisation, but not subsumed by the group mentality. They work at the boundaries, bridges and doorways.

At the edge of the inside of an organisation, a person is "free from its central seductions, but also free to hear its core message in very new and creative ways." Rohr rightly describes this as a prophetic position.

At the edge of inside we can see what's good about the group and what's good about rival groups. Rohr writes:

> "A doorkeeper must love both the inside and the outside of his or her group, and know how to move between these two loves."[83]

I've long held an aversion to insider mentality – in *any* context – with its in-jokes, specialist jargon, cliquey subculture and inward focus that tend to alienate those on the outside.

My commission is first and foremost to love and serve outside the church, while also absolutely recognising the call to be "plugged in" to the spiritual circuitry of Christian community.

The person on the edge of inside, according to Rohr, is involved in a process of perpetual transformation, not a belonging system – more interested in being a searcher than a settler. They neither idolise the *Us* nor demonise the *Them*. Such a person sees different groups as partners in a reality that is paradoxical, complementary and unfolding.

Rohr's explanation of Franciscan spirituality has been of immense value in helping me make sense of something that's been an inherent part of me from the start.

***

---

[83] Richard Rohr. Center for Action and Contemplation: Eight Core Principles. See: https://cac.org/about-cac/missionvision/

We live in an extrovert culture (as Susan Cain, referred to earlier, has very helpfully highlighted in her books), where strong quiet leadership, like that of Jeremy Corbyn, is often overlooked in favour of those who shout the loudest (this has been a party political broadcast on behalf of the Labour Party).

During my first nurse training interview at Eastbourne DGH, I was asked something along the lines of how I would process the emotional challenges of the job; how I would work through the difficult and tragic situations I would inevitably face on the wards.

My answer was that prayer was my strength. As a new Christian, I was freshly aware of the difference prayer made to my life and, as an introvert, solitary prayer had quickly become an instinctive and effective response to life's challenges.

(Remember that the generally accepted key difference between introverts and extroverts is that the former tend to re-energise through solitude and be drained by being social, and vice versa.)

The interviewers didn't seem too happy with my answer. Not because of any kind of anti-faith stance; but as advocates of teamwork they blatantly tried to steer me towards a response around peer support, and virtually put words into my mouth.

They *desperately* wanted me to say that at the end of the week I'd join my colleagues for a drink in the pub and a chinwag over the highs and lows of the working week.

Well, that just wasn't and isn't my style, and I think my honest response that went against the grain of group mentality was another factor that contributed to their rejection first time round.

Again, organisational culture had become the assumed status quo that gave little room for individual differences.

There are dangers and disadvantages to introversion and individualism (just as there are with extraversion or following the pack), some of which I referred to earlier. In one previous workplace I was described as "aloof". It was an entirely understandable perception.

Introverts like me can easily fail to recognise the *need of others* for our participation in their chat. What sometimes looks to me like time-wasting chatter and gossip is in actual fact a pulse for group therapy. With the principle of valuing others' needs above our own at the heart of Christianity, this has been an important lesson that I'm still learning.

In case it seems that I've laboured the point about introversion, I suspect I'm by no means alone (pardon the pun) in finding this to have been a key issue in the whole sphere of self-understanding and finding my place in western society with its particular kind of culture.

However, despite this proclivity towards solitude, coming home to God also entailed a homecoming to *community*.

US hospitality seriously rubbed off on me, stirring something deep in my soul: a sense that homes are for sharing; that the privileges of the well-off exist for the benefit of others, not simply for self-advantage; and that community is a place for inclusion of the excluded, for dynamic diversity in holy disorder.

In Utah I was invited to stay with Mike, who'd picked me up hitch-hiking. Mike was nominally Mormon but claimed to be an active member of 19 different religions! I'm not sure if he collected them like stamps; I tend to think he was eclectic in his taste and, like the guy I hitched a ride with to the Grand Canyon, saw a bigger picture than that presented by any one religion.

As wide as his faith were the doors of his home. He and his wife adopted and fostered kids in addition to having their own; they had about 90 kids staying with them. I might be exaggerating slightly. It was about 8 or 9. The place was full of laughter, wildness, chaos, love.

Mike's heart was big enough to embrace spectrums of faith and kaleidoscopes of kids.

Many others took in this young hitch-hiker, trusting I wasn't going to rob them – or worse. Maybe it was the British accent, maybe they wouldn't have dreamt of taking in a homeless American off the streets – I don't know. I can only speak of my own personal experience and its influence on my future.

People like Mike inspired me, made me feel I wanted to emulate something of their open hearts, their open homes.

Years later, during that period of commitment to singleness while waiting for the right person to come along, it was vital to me that my future wife would share this value, and my prayer was answered in the form of Janine. Over the years we've opened our home to homeless friends, homeless strangers, and friends who just needed a break, and we've hosted a variety of groups full of diverse characters. We've tried in various ways to practise hospitality.

Janine is especially good at welcoming friends old and new into our home, particularly mums with small children, who she'll sometimes be entrusted with caring for. Despite my tidy-freak sensibilities normally being all too easy to ruffle, when I come home from work and find our house littered with toys, toys, toys everywhere, my heart is genuinely warmed to see the messy evidence of healthy hospitality.

Our little daughter Hannah, when she was four years old, boldly declared with a smile, "This is a looking-after house. If you want your children looked after, come to us!" I felt proud that this had been her happy experience.

But I should make it clear that it's now been many years since we've taken in any homeless people, partly because of the professional boundaries associated with my work, partly because we've become more realistic about the risks involved, and I wouldn't necessarily promote the idea of families opening their spare rooms to homeless strangers, many of whom will have complex needs.

The reality is that this kind of hospitality, while commendable, carries too many unknown risks to be a viable option for most people, and may even create a barrier for some rough sleepers to finding the more permanent, personalised solutions that professional agencies will be trying to piece together.

There are other ways of supporting efforts to house the homeless. In many British towns and cities today, housing solutions for homeless people are in short supply and struggle for funding. I would always encourage people to prioritise their support for homeless people, including financial giving, towards organisations that are trying to do this, more than to those that are *just* giving out food and sleeping-bags, although these are often needed too.

Data from the Department for Communities and Local Government revealed Hastings as the local authority with the 9th highest rate of rough sleeping per 1,000 households in England in 2016[84], with appalling rises across the country.

Witnessing this alarming and seemingly unstoppable trend in my own town has given rise to a growing frustration amongst many working with homeless people locally. For Christians at least, this has taken the form of a "holy indignation" that prompted me and a few others from across Hastings and Bexhill churches to set up a new charity, Transom Trust, in 2016.

Transom operates in partnership with national charity Green Pastures, to provide supported housing for homeless people, with pastoral and social care given by volunteers from local churches. The goal of Transom Trust is not only to provide accommodation with social and spiritual support, but a wider, holistic ethos, giving residents opportunities to participate in voluntary work with local social enterprises, thereby building employment skills and self-worth.

In 2017 we established our first flat for two male residents, and in the coming years hope to expand to additional properties.

Details on how to support Transom are given at the end of this book.

For me, this is one way of living out the divine call to hospitality.

But hospitality is not so much about housing homeless people; more a state of mind, an inclusive attitude when it comes to our homes, our social groups, neighbourhoods and other communities. About helping others, especially outsiders, to be at home within *our* spaces, and making our spaces *their* spaces.

---

[84] BBC News, 2017. *Rough sleeping rises at appalling rate*.
http://www.bbc.co.uk/news/uk-england-38719087

My first real experience of coming home to community was outwardly very ordinary. On returning to England in autumn 1987, I took my first ever voluntary step into an English church. Two of the very few Christians I knew were the parents of my school friend Dave B, who were fully involved at Southover Church in Lewes, making it the natural choice to "try out".

It was a typical Anglican building – a dark interior, not helped by the high, stained-glass windows and hardwood pews. There was nothing memorable about the sermons I heard over the roughly 1-year period that I attended the church. In the songs and conversations I sometimes heard a language I didn't understand – no, not the gift of "tongues", just religious English jargon that I wasn't yet accustomed to. The people were friendly and welcoming, but not in any special kind of way.

And yet, the moment I stepped into this very ordinary church on a very ordinary Sunday, I knew immediately that these people were my *family*. My very real family. It wasn't just that they welcomed me in, although they did that. The feeling began even before they'd had a chance to make me feel included, although they did that too, through hospitality, social events, discussion groups and an element of mentoring.

It was much more than any of those things. I felt a *spiritual connection* with these people from the outset – and not just this particular congregation, but with Christians everywhere, although it started here. Not only had I found a sense of belonging in God, and my real identity within the Father's heart, but also community and family with Christians everywhere.

To this day, that feeling remains.

Christians believe that God the Trinity essentially *is community* (three-in-one), and that this community spreads outwards to those who join themselves to him through faith.

People find community in all kinds of places, like the homeless / street community described earlier, and I've found a degree of community with neighbours, in local groups of various kinds, and even through work.

Like any community or family, the church community is flawed – made up of human beings with our ambitions, pride and narrow thinking that cause divisions and disagreements. There's an old cliché that goes, "When you find the perfect church, don't join it, or it'll stop being perfect".

Despite the flaws and the inevitable ups and downs of three decades of church experience, some of which I've tried to portray with honesty and a little humour, as I've reflected with affectionate hindsight on the apparent absurdity of certain episodes, there seems to be a level of trust amongst Christians that's rarely found elsewhere, a sense of belonging and connectedness that runs so much deeper than mere shared interests.

A togetherness that I wouldn't swap for the world. A real feeling of family, and a community in which even this individualist introvert has found a permanent home.

***

My spiritual journey has been patently the most important aspect of my life – the key to who I am and what I do and my transition out of transience. And I'm not the only one who has found a dynamic link between homelessness and faith.

In the first ever study of its kind, Lemos & Crane, a non-faith-based thinktank, conducted in-depth interviews with 75 people attending The Connection day-centre at St Martin-in-the-Fields in London, to explore homeless and ex-homeless people's attitudes towards faith and spirituality.

The report, *Lost and Found*[85], was published in 2013. Its author (and self-described atheist), Carwyn Gravell, reported that, contrary to common assumptions amongst homelessness sector staff who treat faith and spirituality as taboo (often for fear of the unknown, or because they feel uncertain about their own spirituality), matters of faith are close to the heart of many homeless people.

Gravell found that over seventy per cent described themselves as religious or as having been religious at some stage in their lives, and 52% described themselves as being currently religious in the conventional sense.

A further 19% described themselves as religious or spiritual in a broad sense, using terms like this example:

"No specific religious beliefs but I have a deep spiritual outlook."

The study highlighted the importance for homeless or ex-homeless people of coming to terms with the painful experience of loss in the past in order to move forward in their lives.

It describes how some had arrived at a profoundly spiritual perspective on their loss, regarding their present situation free from material ties as being the happiest time of their life, with no desire to return to the world of work and money.

The interviews also revealed that, for some,

"present circumstances (cash-poor but time-rich) were the spur for a rich array of interests, pastimes and blues-beating activities

---

[85] Carwyn Gravell, *Lost and Found*, (London: Lemos and Crane, 2013). https://www.lemosandcrane.co.uk/resources/LostandFound.pdf

that had a strong and timeless spiritual dimension: reading,

music, walking, art and helping others."

This invaluable research emerged from a spirituality discussion group held at the day-centre. Significantly, the group had been instigated *by service users* themselves who, conscious of the day-centre's location next to St Martin's, the iconic Central London church, had raised the idea of a dialogue on faith and spirituality.

Revd. Richard Carter, one of the group's facilitators, comments in the introduction to *Lost and Found*,

"Those who come to the group may not formally identify

themselves as 'religious' or people of 'faith' yet the discussions

that we have had... have been about the very things that are at

the heart of our humanity and are of the essence of spirituality

and faith: hope, joy, forgiveness, suffering, anger, pain, loss,

death, grief, longing, creativity, love, community, healing, life...

"The interviews... reveal clients as individuals seeking to make

meaning of their lives, for themselves and in dialogue with

others...What also comes across is the common search for

integrity, authenticity, and a sense of what can only be described

as the human ability to seek a path which transcends our own

struggles and limitations and become more fully human, and

someone of faith may say more of God."

Sounds familiar.

Far from being a no-go area, most (but not all) of the homeless and ex-homeless people interviewed were more than happy to be asked and to talk about their ideas and beliefs around faith, spirituality and religion, especially when couched within a context of whole life history interviews – again underscoring the value of holism.

The report makes a number of recommendations for agencies supporting homeless people, in terms of recognising and engaging with the spiritual needs of service users.

In my own place of work, we looked at *Lost and Found*, debated its conclusions, which were, interestingly, too controversial for some colleagues who felt intent on preserving the taboo, and eventually formed a few recommendations of our own on how to incorporate spirituality into our service delivery.

Out of that debate was born our own, much smaller, life history project which included the interviews with Jim and Alex referred to earlier, with their accounts and reflections on what had led to their homelessness and the place of hope and meaning in their lives.

***

For me, coming home to me has been clearly and definitively linked with faith in God. For others, self-discovery may happen in different ways. In most cases, though, those moments of "being with", those deeply human-to-human encounters, seem to be pertinent to the process, whether it's people of faith sharing their experiences, counsellors listening in a skilled, empathic way, support workers taking a holistic approach with clients, people taking opportunities to reach out to others in need, or even Grumpy Old Gits chewing the existential cud in Costa. Thorne stated that

> "the more I risk being fully alive the more I will be a transforming companion for my clients and for all those whose lives I touch.... to be human is to be endowed with the spirit of life and to enjoy a

uniqueness which paradoxically links me to my fellow human

beings, my ancestors and the whole of the created order."[86]

However we perceive those interpersonal connections, what could be

better than being present with – being fully alive with – each other on

that voyage of personal and spiritual homecoming, over a mug of coffee?

And perhaps even a dunked sandwich.

[86] Brian Thorne. 1996. *The cost of transparency*. A lecture given to the Annual
General Meeting of the Association for the Person-Centred Approach. University
of East Anglia, Norwich, 15th June 1996.

18: Houses of the holy

A tramp, a gentleman, a poet, a dreamer, a lonely fellow, always hopeful of romance and adventure.

Charlie Chaplin (describing himself)

In Buxted, where I grew up, there were a couple of tramps we saw from time to time. I guess these guys suffered with a mental health disorder, or autism, and didn't fit neatly into mainstream society. They seemed to wander through, sporadically, like ragged spirits. I've no idea why they'd turn up every so often, tramping along the main road, or where they'd been in the meantime. As a child I never thought about it.

I'd love to know the story behind those characters now: their childhoods, dreams, struggles, their thoughts on life. Perhaps, like many homeless people today, there was trauma or tragedy behind their lives on the move.

But there's also an ancient association between itinerancy and *spirituality*, a travelling lifestyle serving as suitable means for the widespread distribution of a pastor's, preacher's or prophet's message, especially before the days of electronic or even postal communication. A far more personal touch.

Itinerant ministry has been closely linked with religious asceticism, with the practice of travelling light and dependence on divine provision. The idea of moving about with little more than trust in God played a part in my own journey to faith, as I became increasingly curious to test out whether "God", if he was there, would provide on my travels when I had nothing on my back.

Travelling ministry, in Christian traditions, is characterised by intentional dependence on human hospitality, opening the way for those heart-to-heart, soul-to-soul connections in people's homes, those "being with"s, that I believe are so close to God's heart for his children.

It's therefore not surprising that Jesus chose homelessness, not out of any psychological damage or disconnection like me; rather, to forge those human/human, human/divine connections and bring *healing* to his hosts' psychological dysfunctionality and physical brokenness.

Nor is it surprising that he sent his disciples out on the same kind of missions to bring healing and wholeness.

Man connecting with man. God connecting with man.

People becoming reconnected with themselves by connecting with God.

Jesus chose homelessness also because he sided with the marginalised, the weak, the despised, the poor, the "sinners". He chose a lifestyle that would demonstrate solidarity with them.

"The son of man has nowhere to lay his head."

His mother's accounts of his homeless birth must have echoed prophetically in his head as he figured out his Father's calling to live a life of identification with the poor.

And, as he went about his transient ministry, he searched out people, mostly the kinds excluded by the religious authorities of his day, who would take him into their homes to share a meal, benefitting both them and him. He created those mutual "being with"s, not always even waiting to be invited.

Such was his zeal to heal that social airs and graces sometimes went out the proverbial window. Like the time he invited himself to the house of the notorious tax-collector Zaccheus, creating a scene of celebration and forgiveness, to the chagrin of the shocked religious onlookers.

This was the equivalent of Jesus today celebrating with Pride revellers in full view of a crowd of American fundamentalists.

Jesus felt at home in other people's homes. By moving about and entering the houses of the poor, eating, talking and praying with them, he gave them a sense of acceptance and worth and dignity – bringing healing to bodies, minds, human divisions and disconnections.

In so doing Jesus created a homecoming for both him and them.

I believe he still does that, his life on earth reflecting the eternal God – the itinerant Spirit who searches out hearts to make a home in and turns ordinary people into houses of the holy[87].

I learned early on in this spiritual journey that if we want to see God, a good place to start looking is in the faces of the poor.

The Jewish prophets of long ago, like Solomon and Isaiah, and Christian apostles like James and John, not to mention Jesus himself[88], all concurred that if we mock the poor or ignore their plight, if we fail to take care of the needs of the broken, the rejected, the vulnerable, then we mock or ignore God, and all our worship services are useless.

Just as Isaiah describes those who are homeless, hungry or in some other way destitute as our own flesh and blood, Jesus similarly identifies them as his brothers and sisters and even his representatives. Whatever we do to them – help or ignore – we do to him.

---

[87] A nod to Led Zeppelin, *Houses of the Holy* (album), Atlantic, 1973.
[88] For example: Proverbs 17:5; Isaiah 58:6-12; James 1:27; Matthew 25:31-46.

As I delved into the Christians' book, I discovered almost from the start the Bible's claims that if we want to know God's identity, then we need to look into the faces of those who are crying out for our help – these houses of the holy – often a silent cry from deep within their hearts, but which can be heard by those with a trace of human empathy and compassion. There is so much to love about Christian spirituality.

***

One of the first quotes of Jesus I ever heard, that made sense of my own conversion, was the time when he talked about himself and the Father making their home with his followers.

One of his disciples had asked how come he was making himself known to them and not to the rest of the world. Christians still sometimes make the same mistake – they ask the wrong question, assuming that Jesus is only for people who call themselves Christians and the rest of the world is godless.

Jesus' reply, as always, is astounding: "*Anyone* who loves me will obey my teaching. My Father will love them, and we will come to them and make our home with them" [89] (italics mine), putting the emphasis once again on living a life based on his teaching, rather than claiming to belong to a certain religion, as the evidence of loving him. And on that basis, there is a homecoming for God in the heart of anyone who lives out his teachings. From the beginning of my spiritual awakening and in my return to England to live out this faith, I felt so strongly, not only that I had come home, but astonishingly that *God* had come home to *me*, to live within *my* life. It was a revelatory, game-changing thought.

---

[89] John 14:23.

The church, or Christianity, had never had any appeal, nothing that ever resembled a comfortable home to flop into. But this has never been about religion. From my very first prayer, this has been about a faith in the Source of all Life, who fills the Universe – and human hearts.

But Jesus spoke not just of a homecoming for him and the Father, but of a home-*making*. Over the years I've come to understand that Jesus is not looking for blind obedience to a book, but for hearts that will make space for *him*.

Perhaps this works differently for other people, but for me it means engaging in stillness, being mindfully conscious of his beauty not only in the people and the world around me but also in myself with my own brokenness, choosing to trust his absolute acceptance over my criticism of me and others. Jesus seems to set up home in that kind of heart.

Perhaps above all, for me, it's meant focussing on the direct teachings of Jesus and tuning in my heart to the things that consume his heart, which sometimes stand in contrast to the (*perceived*) obsessions of the established church.

Thankfully, the (sometimes) public perception of Christianity, as a self-seeking, patriarchal faith obsessed with issues of sexuality and outdated gender inequality, is not what I see in the reality of the church where I live. Instead, I see multitudes of Christians from all denominations sharing my leanings towards a faith lived out in love-filled action – Jesus' passion for social justice, peacemaking, overcoming hatred with love, identifying with the poor. Those things that first grabbed my attention as an atheist who dared to peek into the Gospel of Matthew increasingly consume my heart. I'm by no means alone.

And, through this engagement with Jesus' agenda, I sense a melding of hearts, of Jesus and the Father being at home in this very human heart, in spite of my hang-ups, failings and even hypocrisy.

19: My beautiful launderette

(returning to homeland)

Heaven above is softer blue,

Earth around is sweeter green;

Something lives in every hue

Christless eyes have never seen

George Wade Robinson (Irish 19th Century poet) – *Loved with*

Everlasting Love

In 1985, *My Beautiful Laundrette* courageously handled the hot potatoes of its time: racism, immigration, sexuality, homophobia, materialism and the cash obsessed entrepreneurialism of the 80s against a backdrop of struggling Thatcherite Britain with its gaping race- and class-divides. Despite the big hair and flamboyant clothes, the film is as pertinent to 2017 Britain as it was in its time.

The plot centres on a young British man of Pakistani descent who employs his white friend, thereby turning the established race tables, in order to transform a run-down dive of a launderette into a centre of glamour, a launderette that people would be drawn to – and would therefore make money.

The memory I have of a launderette shortly after the film's release, in the period between my two trips to the USA, bears more resemblance to the former, grittier, version of the launderette in the film than its second incarnation.

A small incident, but one that epitomised my then dim view of Britain.

After my relationship with Helen, and therefore my life, had fallen apart, I'd moved back down to Lewes, where I lived in a state of semi-permanent stoned-ness, saving up to step back out on the road.

It was a typical, drizzly, English winter's afternoon, the skies and streets as grey and grim as my feelings about England, when I took my washing to the local launderette. On this dismal day, a young man pushed right past me and shoved his washing in the dryer, just as I was about to dry mine, clearly and knowingly jumping the queue. I'd already staked my claim on that dryer by placing my coins atop the machine.

Yeah, I'm still bitter after all these years! No, not really.

It was a minor infraction of social etiquette, hardly a heinous crime. But that day, that moment, this brief encounter was for me a microcosm of all that was wrong with the country I was unfortunate enough to have been brought up in – a clear glimpse into the wider societal gloom and a symptom of a selfish culture, where everyone was out to take whatever they could get, with no respect for anyone else. (My hypocrisy in this matter, and the irony of it, didn't occur to me!)

This would never have happened in the States, I thought, where sunnier climes matched the people's attitudes – where generosity and friendliness abounded. Like the Beach Boys, I couldn't wait to get back[90].

Our perception of places is so tainted by our own subjective experiences and psychological state that two people living in the same town or country might just as well be in entirely different places, to hear their perspectives on where they live. Nowhere is that contrast more striking than here in Hastings.

---

[90] Beach Boys, *California Girls,* Capitol, 1965.

For many people Hastings, with its more-than-fair share of green spaces to explore and get lost in, comfortingly bounded by the sea's symphonic movements, is a wonderfully quirky town, brimming with art and character(s) and life. That's how I feel.

For others, Hastings is a dead-end town, full of alkies and junkies, with few job prospects and poor travel links to London and the rest of the world. "Why would anyone want to live here?" they might scoff.

To bring Irvin Yalom into this again: in a chapter on empathy[91], the renowned psychotherapist gives an enlightening example of how two people may see the same situation quite differently.

He tells of a female patient who had looked forward to her naysaying father driving her to college, seeing the time together as an opportunity for their reconciliation. On the journey, however, he behaved true to form, moaning continually about the polluted, littered creek by the roadside, while all she could see was a beautiful, unspoiled, rustic stream. His negative attitude towards something so lovely left her unable to know how to respond to him and they continued the trip in silence.

Later, making the journey alone, she was astounded to discover there were *two* streams, one on each side. The stream on the driver's side of the car was just as polluted and ugly as her father had described it. By this time, it was too late and her father was dead and buried.

Yalom uses this example to remind his students and himself to

> "Look out the other's window. Try to see the world as your patient sees it."

---

[91] Irvin Yalom, *The Gift of Therapy* (London: Piatkus, 2002), 18.

Empathy is a vital quality for those of us supporting homeless and other vulnerable people, whose life stories are usually a million miles from anything we've ever known. And even if we have shared some similar experiences, the sum total of who we are and all our life's encounters creates for each of us an entirely unique perspective on reality.

I remember another laundry-room encounter, this time in my post-conversion days, in the 1990s. Some friends and I had been doing some church outreach into Ennersdale House in Hither Green, South East London, just ¼ mile from where I lived. 28p Jonny had lived there for a while.

This enormous, direct-access hostel had recently undergone a major refurbishment after changing hands from the local authority to housing association, scaling down from shared dormitories accommodating 192 homeless men to single rooms for 117. Although still barely manageable with such large numbers of people with complex needs, it had been a huge improvement.

This particular evening I'd got chatting with a 40-something-year-old resident in the nicely refurbished laundry-room of the hostel. I'd talked, not too condescendingly I thought, about how things had changed for me since becoming a Christian. Whatever I'd said, or how I'd said it, had wound him up, as he snapped at me: "What do you see around you? A nice new laundry-room? Well, I see a shit-hole!" and he stormed off.

Of course. For me, the hostel seemed like an all right place to live. Better than being on the streets. For him, life was probably pretty "shit" and his surroundings perpetually reflected that view back on him. Despite the improvements at Ennersdale House, this was no doubt the last place he wanted to be. Perhaps, in becoming homeless, he had lost a family, a life, an identity...

What did I know? I knew nothing of his life. How arrogant of me to begin to tell him what I thought he needed. I hadn't even begun to attempt to look at the world through his eyes.

To put ourselves in the shoes of homeless people and *look out* through their eyes, rather than simply trying to *look into* their lives, is a hard – and inestimable – skill to hone. I've had the good fortune to have known a few exceptional friends and colleagues to whom this seems to come as a (super)natural gift, and I'm envious of them in the nicest possible way. To be understood in this way, to know that someone's identified with you to this depth, is a most incredible, healing gift.

One of the huge appeals of the Christian faith is just that: the idea that someone with all the privilege and power of God chose to put himself in the tattered shoes of humanity and undergo the whole spectrum of human emotion, rejection, anguish and desolation, culminating at his death on the cross.

Again, the appeal of Christianity is more than beliefs and ideas, our faith extending to an *experiential knowledge* of that divine empathy, deep in our core, as the Holy Spirit brings the reality of Christ into the realm of everyday experience. The sense that Christ sees the world through our eyes and is with us in our world.

Brian Thorne, commenting on the full humanity of Jesus, puts it this way:

> "Jesus is open to the full range of existential torment. He knows what it means to feel utterly desperate, abandoned by the God in whom he had placed his complete trust. He knows what it means

to grasp the hope which lies beyond despair and to trust again against all reason."[92]

This is what we Christians mean by the comfort of Christ; a strengthening of the soul that's engendered by receiving communion or reflecting on the cross, through the prayers of another, or simply through our daily walk of faith; it's something I prize highly, that motivates me in my work as I strive to emulate Christ's empathy.

***

So in that not-so-beautiful Lewes launderette in '86, I despised this scepter'd isle and was once again eager to escape back on to the roads of far-flung continents. Now I love my country; and I see my homeland through very different eyes.

But here's a funny thing...

As I write this, the world is reeling from the aftermath of President Trump's inauguration. Here in the UK, people are shocked at Trump's pronouncements, devastated by the potential effects his policies will have on the world, not just America. And like many others, I find "America First" a somewhat sickening, self-serving slogan that flies against the ideal of loving one's neighbour as oneself.

However...

On my second trip around the USA in 1987, I was *impressed* by the patriotism of many Americans I hitched rides with. I don't mean those arrogant nationalist, or fascist, claims that the USA is somehow better or more important than other countries, nor the Trumpish idea that only America and its citizens matter. I mean the pride that these people took in

---

[92] Brian Thorne, *Behold The Man* (London: Darton, Longman & Todd, 2006).

their country; their positive attitude towards their nation, in contrast with the cynical, negative view of the typical Brit towards his home country. I suppose it was part and parcel of the more upbeat characteristic of the American population generally.

This wasn't what drew me back to Britain, but it very definitely rubbed off on me. It was all part of the call back to my homeland.

A new love for England developed; a sense that this was my home, my place to be. The homecoming in the core of my soul rippled outwards in concentric rings, extending to my attitude towards the country of my birth. Contempt for England turned to love.

Although there may be many good reasons for citizens of even western countries emigrating in search of a better life, I've also seen plenty of people look for external solutions to internal problems. In my case, the need to escape was cured by an inner peace, and although there are places in the world I'd like to visit, I have no strong urge to go anywhere. Geographical restlessness was defeated by finding my spiritual home. Through the whole initial transition in '87 from hedonist to God-worshipper, taker to(wards) giver, there emerged a clear sense of *calling* back to England. I felt absolutely driven to give what I had towards meeting the practical and spiritual needs of people in my own country. Like the Blues Brothers, I was on a mission from God! Only, slightly more seriously.

But, although the world suddenly no longer revolved around me, my heart was also filled with an almost inexplicable, newfound attraction towards these fair isles for my own delight.

***

At home I have a painting of the South Downs. In one corner, by a stream, stands a single, solitary, yellow iris; it's always seemed out-of-place to me. Superfluous, against the subtle, graduating shades of green and grey that make up the rest of the picture: dull hues beautiful in their own right, that have no need of gaudy flowers to supplement their understated splendour.

I'll never forget New Year's Day 1988 – my first new year as a new person. Everything was different, felt different, even *looked* different.

Instead of partying New Year's Eve, I'd gone to bed about 10pm, before an early start for a hike on the Downs. I left the house about 6am, with the aim of watching the sun rise, and headed out from the old Lewes racecourse, along the ridge of downland overlooking Plumpton, taking in 17 miles of chalk-strewn path (not a long walk for me back then; out of my range these days!).

There was no sunrise, no dawn to be seen. Just a very gradual shifting of tones, as my nocturnal surroundings slowly gave way to breathtaking landscapes in dull, cloud-laden shades of green and grey, like an unveiling of a rarely seen masterpiece.

I'd never appreciated the Downs like I did that morning. Just two months earlier, I'd enjoyed the hike down to the base of the Grand Canyon – infinitely more colourful, *obvious* in its beauty, almost brash, like the British perception of America as a whole, in comparison with Sussex. This New Year's Day, the Grand Canyon had nothing on the South Downs. *Nothing.*

In the words of Lou Reed, it was "a perfect day"[93].

---

[93] Lou Reed, *Perfect Day*, RCA, 1972.

Of course, the Grand Canyon *is* magnificent. And even in that tourist trap I found peace and solitude, overnighting there in the canyon's base.

But the Downs apprehended my aesthetic preference in such a profound way because this was *home*. Not only that, but what the South Downs lack in comparison with the Canyon's sheer size, power and explosive colour, they make up for in gentle femininity.

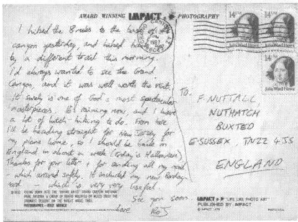

A postcard I sent to my Dad on Halloween 1987, after a night in the Canyon
— probably my first ever written acknowledgement of God

The naturalist-writer William Henry Hudson wrote that "during the whole fifty-three mile length from Beachy Head to Harting the ground never rises above a height of 850 feet, but we feel on top of the world."

I can understand the attraction to mighty mountains and the challenge of "conquering" them. The Downs are different. They don't stand defiantly, as a masculine opponent to be defeated; instead, they invite the walker, the pray-er, the mystic, the lover, into a warm, maternal embrace – the arms of Mother Nature, shielding her children from the torrents of the world.

The spiritual homecoming – God at home in me, me at home in God – had completely changed my outlook on England, Sussex, its people and countryside.

And this New Year's Day was yet another important homecoming milestone – a newfound appreciation of my home country, my Home County.

I came across the painting in a Lewes High Street shop a few months later. It captured that New Year's Day scene perfectly (apart from the unnecessary iris!). We were meant for each other. It was the first painting I ever bought.

Nothing could compete with the Downs ever again. Even today, I have this routine with my wife whenever we visit some beautiful landscape. I'll say "It's OK, but not as nice as the Downs," and she'll roll her eyes at me. She might think it's a standing joke, but I'm not even joking...

20: A life backwards

Life can only be understood backwards; but it must be lived forwards.
Soren Kierkegaard

As a typical teenager, my bedroom walls were plastered with music posters, mostly ripped out of trashy pop magazines: everything from the Sex Pistols to Grease (I wasn't *that* punk), and of course pictures of female pop stars, like Toyah and Kim Wilde – schoolboy fantasies of the time, all those years ago.

Music was one of my escapes and the vicarious voice of teenage turmoil. As well as posters, I had song lyrics, pulled from the pages of *Smash Hits*, Blu-Tacked on to my wall, like the words from UB40's *Don't Let It Pass You By*[94] that urged me, in the absence of God, heaven, hell or any kind of afterlife, to make the most of *this* life.

The song gave perfect expression to my atheist worldview and resolve not to waste my life on the meaningless drudgery of the rat-race.

Although some claim to be atheist and might say that this physical life is all there is, I think the majority of people, whether spiritual, religious or otherwise, tend to feel some inner sense that death *isn't* in fact the end. One spiritual writer observed that we are born with two diseases: life, from which we die; and hope, which says that the first disease is not terminal.

The various world faiths have come up with all kinds of concepts like paradise, reincarnation / nirvana, spiritualism and heaven, to express that

---

[94] UB40, *Don't Let It Pass You By*, DEP International, 1981.

human hope and longing for an answer to the very human problem of death.

One ancient Jewish writer claimed that

"He has also set eternity in the human heart; yet no one can fathom what God has done from beginning to end."[95]

As a Christian, you might expect me to have certain, clear beliefs about heaven but, to be honest, like that Jewish writer I haven't a clue!

And I'm not sure that Jesus, arriving on the scene a few hundred years after the quote above and speaking in parables and metaphors, made eternity any more fathomable, despite claiming to come from God.

Which I think is because we're talking about a reality beyond the reach of human words or concepts. Lao Tzu summarised the situation like this:

"He who knows does not speak; he who speaks does not know."

However, there are one or two things about eternity that seem planted in my spirit, more intuitive than intellectual, though rooted nevertheless in Judeo-Christian tradition.

The first is that heaven is the ultimate *home* – where life's pilgrims will finally be able to hang their boots.

The homecoming process I've been enjoying since '87 ain't over and can only reach its conclusion beyond this world.

That literary comic genius Adrian Plass gave this description of home:

"I just wanted to go home. I wanted to be in the place where I really belonged, where I slotted into a shape that was my shape, a perfect fit through constant use."[96]

---

[95] Ecclesiastes 3:11
[96] Adrian Plass, *View From A Bouncy Castle* (London: Fount, 1991).

Whatever afterlife there may be (and I'm *sure* there'll be no floating on clouds with harps), Plass' turn-of-phrase sounds to me like a fitting description of the destination shared by people of faith through countless ages: the goal of our movement, where we were always meant to be, a place to be free, be "me", beyond the constraints we place on ourselves and each other.

In the brilliant classic *Astral Weeks*[97] Van Morrison sang of having a home on high, in another place.

And yet, although there is something "beyond" and "other" about this ultimate home that defies temporal concepts, I hold to the other Jewish / Christian idea that heaven really will be *a place on earth*; I embrace a hope and belief in the renewal of our weary world with its battered environment.

The splendour of places like the South Downs seems to provide a glimpse into that future paradise.

***

My other gut feeling about that realm reflects the sentiments of Biblical characters Mary (mother of Jesus) and Hannah (Samuel's mother), who sang of fortunes being reversed for both downtrodden and downtreaders. After receiving a foretaste of that other-world justice, both maternal prophets sang as if that day was already a reality. Faith sees fragments of the future breaking into the present.

In the fullness of that future, we believe not so much that the world is turned upside-down but that our topsy-turvy society is turned *the right way up*.

---

[97] Van Morrison, *Astral Weeks*, from the album *Astral Weeks*, Warner Bros, 1968.

In the months leading up to my conversion in '87, U2 hit no.1 in the US charts with *I Still Haven't Found What I'm Looking For*[98] which, despite many Christians missing the point at the time and wondering if Bono et al had lost their faith, vocalised the ache felt by those who hear the Father's heartbeat for justice and *right*ness which can never be satisfied in this battle-torn world.

Our perspectives on this world are inclined to be upside-down, back-to-front, inside-out, simply because of the limitations of our humanness. Faith gives us glimmers of the bigger picture, hope of a better future. Although our clouded, human thinking means that we cannot "fathom what God has done from beginning to end", human lives are often a little more fathomable *from end to beginning*.

Our lives make a whole lot more sense in reverse.

For a very long time, I understood my life the wrong way round. That is, I (naturally) assumed that I'd been drawn towards supporting homeless people after having developed an affinity with the street community in my younger days of self-appointed vagrancy.

But in light of the *destiny* that I feel running through my veins, I now tend to see my life backwards – or rather the right way round. This is what I was always meant to do, who I was meant to be. This is not a happy by-product of a negative past. Each of us has our own small part to play in making the world a better place, each in our own very different, individual ways. This was my part from the start.

I wrote at the beginning of this book that "life on the road was an unusual ambition for a young, middle-class boy" and went on to recount some of

---

[98] U2, *I Still Haven't Found What I'm Looking For*, Island, 1987.

the childhood experiences that, from a human, psychological perspective, fed the need for that kind of freedom.

This *is* true on one level. But on a higher level, *the cause and effect are the other way round*: my longing for life on the road and streets was *because* of a predetermined vocation to support and be alongside homeless people. It was all part of the call.

Every twist and turn of early years was building up to what I do now. Lavoisier's conclusion that "Nothing is lost...everything is transformed" can be as true of human lives as of chemistry.

What does this mean for me and for the people I work with?

For me, it gives a greater confidence in what I do. That's not to say arrogance – I have no delusions of always getting things right – but it does mean in those times of self-doubt and negative thinking that plague me, and especially when I get things wrong, that I can tap into that restful assurance that I'm the right person in the right place, with access to every spiritual resource I need to help me do what I do.

"Seeing backwards" in this sense opens the way to an alternative perspective on other people's lives too. Seeing backwards unleashes imagination for unseen potential; discovers endless possibilities for the futures of vulnerable people.

One of the funniest, saddest and most honest portraits of homelessness I've come across is *Stuart: A Life Backwards*[99], a bestselling first book by Alexander Masters, tracing the life of Stuart Shorter, "a mentally unstable, knife-wielding thief" – starting at age 32 and looking back over his life at

---

[99] *Stuart: A Life Backwards,* Alexander Masters (London: Harper Collins, 2006).

the chain of events that moulded and shaped the man – told "backwards" on Stuart's own insistence.

At age 33, Stuart's life was cut short when he walked in front of a train. It might therefore be hard to argue that he fulfilled his hidden potential. But there are *degrees* of recovery, degrees of self-actualisation; and, despite the apparent suicide (the jury returned an open verdict), he demonstrated incredible fortitude in attenuating the lasting effects of childhood abuse that seemed to overshadow his life.

Rather than lie down and play the all-too-easy role of victim, Stuart became a staunch activist for the homeless, presenting a BBC documentary, *Private Investigations*, denouncing police plans to ban homeless people from Cambridge city centre, before becoming a leading figure in the campaign to release Ruth Wyner and John Brock, Director and Day Centre Manager of Wintercomfort for the Homeless, who had been sent to prison after some of the people they were supporting had been secretly dealing drugs on the charity's premises. The campaign ended in the release of the "Cambridge Two" after just six months.

Fragments of the future breaking into the present. Not just in the shape of justice for Wyner and Brock, but in the reversal of role for Stuart, from victim of abuse to campaigning activist and freedom-fighter. A friend of true justice, who set things right by turning tables upside-down and living life backwards.

The world – my world – is a better place when it's upside-down and back to front.

21: Son to father

*To understand and reconnect with our stories, the stories of the
ancestors, is to build our identities.*
Frank Delaney

Speculation over hypothetical, alternative scenarios isn't necessarily a bad
thing. "What if...?"s can make us grateful for the way things *did* turn out.
Looking back to my first escape from home and subsequent hitch back to
Buxted on my way to Brighton from London: if the police hadn't turned up
at that moment – those few minutes I'd stopped at home to collect some
belongings – I wonder how things would have transpired. One thing I'm
sure of is that I would have completed my plan and made it to my
destination, to sleep rough.

Would I have been another teenage runaway statistic on the streets of
Brighton? Would I have had any clue how to survive on the streets as a
naive 16-year-old from a sheltered, privately-educated background?
Hardly. What kind of life would I have drifted into?

Apart from the obvious tendency of homeless people to mollify their grim
reality with alcohol and other drugs, there is the insidious effect of
homelessness on mental health.

There is a theory that within just 3 weeks of being on the streets,
homeless people develop a coping mechanism akin to a mental health
disorder. The "three-week rule" describes the period during which people
readily adapt to homelessness in order to survive, and after which it is
more difficult to integrate back into mainstream society: a pattern which

has been observed particularly amongst young people with a history of running away.

A staff member at a Manchester day centre commented:

> "After about three weeks they stop being angry about their situation and accept it; at the same time they stop being able to do anything about it."[100]

It's easy to see, then, how easily rough sleepers become "entrenched" in their lifestyle – a word often used in the context of homelessness to describe the rapid slide into an intractable situation.

It's also the reasoning behind the Government initiatives *No One Left Out* and *No Second Night Out* in recent years. Sadly, these (perhaps well-meaning) strategies have been vastly under-resourced and (the latter) focussed only on selected areas of the country.

The intention of the 2008 policy *No One Left Out* was to end rough sleeping by 2012 – an ambitious aim! On the contrary, with no real, tangible or financial commitment by our austerity-focussed Tory government to tackle homelessness, rough sleeping has risen dramatically across the country since then, with major increases in some areas.

Today, Brighton – 40 miles down the coast from Hastings where I live and work – has the second highest rate of homelessness in the country, with shocking numbers of rough sleepers lining its streets. In fact, recent figures show that 1 in 69 people in Brighton is homeless.[101]

---

[100] Crisis. 1996. Still dying for a home. http://www.crisis.org.uk/publications-search.php?fullitem=234

[101] "One in 69 people in Brighton and Hove is homeless". 1/12/16. *The Argus*. http://www.theargus.co.uk/news/14939514.One_in_69_people_in_Brighton_an_d_Hove_is_homeless/

And that's not even including the "hidden homeless", sleeping on friends' sofas. The city is now rich with services, struggling to find adequate solutions against a rising tide of homelessness, extortionate housing prices and the longstanding popularity of the city as a destination for travellers, day-trippers and the transient.

I don't know how homeless services worked back in the early '80s, but if I were in the same situation as a young person on the streets of Brighton today, the likelihood is that outreach workers would pick me up and try to reconnect me with my parents.

Under current housing law, local authority housing services have to apply 5 legal "tests" to each homeless application: 5 hoops that a homeless person has to jump through, in order to be accepted for emergency housing assistance.

Most of the homeless people I meet fail at least one of these tests.

When I first started to work professionally in the homelessness field, it came as quite a shock to learn that state housing services operate within a legal system, under which many homeless people are denied assistance due to strict legal criteria. It's second nature to healthcare professionals like me to provide a service to anyone and everyone who needs it without discrimination, as it is for most people who deliver any kind of service.

One of those 5 hoops is Local Connection. The homeless applicant needs to be able to demonstrate that they have lived in the local authority area for 6 out of the last 12 months or 3 out of the last 5 years, or fulfil certain other criteria related to close family members or employment.

State-funded homeless services will normally try to reconnect rough sleepers from out of the area to the district or borough where they do have a legal local connection, for housing assistance by the local authority there.

This process works occasionally, but for many there's a good reason for not being in their "home" area. They may be fleeing domestic violence, some perceived or actual threat, or they may be escaping a place associated with traumatic or unhappy memories. They may simply feel in need of a fresh start in a new place.

Not everyone wants to be "reconnected" in this sense, just as not everyone wants to be rehabilitated, as the late Amy Winehouse expressed so tragically in *Rehab*[102].

There is a kind of longing for reconnection within the soul of every man and woman, though, which Christianity claims to be able to fulfil.

You could say that Christianity is all about reconnection – with God and self, rippling outwards into reconciliation with others. In fact, the very root of the word *religion* is thought to mean re-ligation: or re-joining together, a healing of disjointedness. Peace with God translated into peace with self and others.

But the spiritual life doesn't always happen in any defined order, that is, the way sometimes prescribed or anticipated by religion.

As that spiritual master Jesus explained, or rather didn't explain, this mystery to a religious "expert", Nicodemus:

> "The wind blows wherever it wants. Just as you can hear the wind but can't tell where it comes from or where it is going, so you can't explain how people are born of the Spirit."[103]

---

[102] Amy Winehouse, *Rehab*, Island, 2006.
[103] Gospel of John, Chapter 3.

My reconnection, or reconciliation, with my Dad happened on my journey to faith but while I was still essentially an atheist. You might think it would have happened the other way round. And my Dad wasn't even there.

At the time the extraordinary event seemed purely random, but after conversion I had no doubt of the Holy Spirit's instigation.

It was an unremarkable evening at the end of an unremarkable day's hitch-hiking, a few months into my travels in the USA in '87. I'd made a small camp-fire, as was my custom, on which I'd cooked a basic meal. Beans and noodles – something like that.

The fire had simmered down and the chirping of the crickets was the only sound in this desolate patch of dust in the middle of mid-west nowhere, as I entered my little 2-man tent for the night.

Suddenly, for no reason I could have figured at the time (I hadn't particularly been thinking about him), I was overcome with incredible remorse for the selfish and hateful ways I'd treated my Dad over the years.

Coupled with regret for my own actions and attitudes, I was filled with forgiveness towards *him*, in an instant realising that Dad had only ever tried his best for me, that like me he was human, imperfect and had made forgivable mistakes.

My relationship with him was healed in an out-of-the-blue moment. That evening in my tent changed things forever between the two of us.

I had no faith in God yet, but like the wind the Holy Spirit was blowing in unexpected directions.

I already mentioned Nancy's observation that, on my second visit to her in LA, I seemed alive in a way I hadn't been before. My Dad said something similar.

Having returned to England a new person a few months after the forgiveness encounter in the tent, it took me several weeks, because of the relational distance we'd had between us, to summon the courage to give Dad the profound, personal news that I'd "become a Christian".

His response was one of *some* delight (I think) but little surprise, having already witnessed the visible change. I've never forgotten his exact words: "Your whole demeanour has changed."

No doubt, this was an observation of my reformed attitude towards him in particular as well as my new perspective on the world in general.

Bearing in mind his own previous reneging on Christianity some 25 years earlier, it's hard to know quite what he made of his young son's conversion! On the one hand, he could see signs of something obviously positive before his very eyes; on the other, I think he must have inevitably borne some residual suspicion, if not antipathy, towards religion.

If he did have mixed feelings, it didn't alter the fact that our relationship was permanently reconciled.

I felt like the Prodigal Son on more than one level – like I'd lived out the parable both in its intended meaning (coming home to God the Father) and literally.

In subsequent years, Dad would occasionally voice the question that had lingered in his mind from his long-gone faith and formed one of the main barriers between him and a return to Christianity: "How can a loving God allow so much suffering?"

I've learned over the years that this common conundrum often belies a person's own personal grief rather than a general objection to faith; that the asker may be voicing a deep need for comfort, empathy and understanding in relation to their own experience of suffering, rather than theoretical, theological answers.

Nobody wants glib answers to sensitive, complex problems.

This was almost certainly true in Dad's case. Not only had he suffered the painful loss of his first wife; he'd also lived and fought through the Second World War as an RAF air gunner, witnessing and surviving the deaths of many friends. The repercussions of these events had undoubtedly taken a hidden, emotional toll on him over the years.

I don't think I ever matured enough in Dad's lifetime to appreciate the depth of his bereavements or the price he'd paid long before I was born to ensure our present-day liberty: a typical father-son relationship expressed so well by Brian May in *Father to Son*[104].

Nor, I think, did I ever make any serious and personalised attempt to answer his question of suffering. On top of this, in my young evangelical fervour, I inadvertently irritated him with my Bible-bashing and attempts to re-convert him!

Nevertheless, he was forgiving about all of this, and our relationship grew from strength to strength, from my return to the UK in 1987 until his death in 2006.

Dad was old school. Born in 1920, he was fairly typical of his generation – stiff-upper-lipped Brit, firm on traditional values. Shirt and tie till the day he died.

As our relationship developed over the years, I learned to appreciate his sense of dignity, of honour, honesty and chivalry. Although he and I were very different, I hope I caught something of those values.

---

[104] Queen, *Father to Son*, from the album *Queen II*, EMI, 1974.

Dad may not have been an expert at putting himself in the shoes of others or steering his two families emotionally through the difficult twists and turns of life, other than to put on a brave face, but these are challenging qualities to gain, which many struggle with. Unfortunately, such stoical determination can have long-term negative consequences for both the person and those around them.

But I've also learned that stoicism isn't *always* such a bad thing.

***

One Sunday evening I visited our local winter night shelter, which opens for 4 months of the year, from November to March. It was the penultimate night of the season, and as I chatted with some of the homeless visitors, I was nervous about asking them what they were going to do when Tuesday morning came around and there would be no more night shelter for another 8 months.

I was anticipating heart-rending replies along the lines of "I haven't got a clue. I'll probably die on the street", and was worried I'd feel at a loss for anything remotely useful to say in response.

However, I *did* ask, and contrary to my expectations one single lady in her 40s told me with a big, determined smile, "It's OK. I've bought a tent. I have a sleeping-bag. It's going to be fine."

"How can that be fine?" I thought. "You're a vulnerable, single woman, who's going to sleep out alone."

But of course I smiled and nodded and went along with her stoic resolve. Faced with no other choice than to sleep rough, what better way to deal with a desperate situation than to make the best of it, put on a smile and face it head on with a positive attitude. That's survival.

People tend to derive resilience from having just such a positive attitude, sense of humour and social capital: that is, support from peers, family, friends and even professionals. Resilient people bounce back from misfortune, often stronger than before.

I've seen and admired incredible resilience amongst homeless people, and this was a perfect example.

And as for me, this sensitive soul, I'm learning that sometimes I too need to simply put on some steadfast determination to get through all the challenges of work and life.

***

Stoic resolve was the only way my Dad knew to survive the traumas of his life. No counselling, no tears, no tea and sympathy for him.

When I moved to Hastings in 2004, wrenching my young family away from our amazing network of friends in London, it was firstly to take up the work I do now with a homeless health service. But it was also to be nearer Dad, who had recently moved into a care home with progressing dementia.

Dementia is often described as a cruel disease, as people see their loved one's memories, personality and identity slip away before their eyes. Losing the mother, father, sister, brother they love, while that person is still physically there.

Although there was an element of that with Dad, he never lost recognition of his children, and our relationship grew closer rather than distant.

The disinhibition often associated with dementia, in his case, increasingly softened his way of relating to people. Never having been one for hugs – we shook hands in previous years – his eyes lit up whenever I visited him in the care home, and he'd wrap his arms around me. An increase in physical affection was a welcome symptom of Dad's advancing illness. After some less successful placements, Dad settled cheerfully into Mount Denys, a County Council-run nursing home that specialised in dementia, where the staff loved him, and he them. To be fair, he was always a bit of a charmer with the ladies, and at this particular home he hit it off with the predominantly female staff.

Dad passed away peacefully at Mount Denys on 13th October 2006. It was strange but I felt virtually no sorrow – for three reasons that I could see: first, we'd already lost him gradually through his illness; secondly, he'd ended his days genuinely contented; lastly, and perhaps of greatest significance, I think I lacked sorrow because of the peace and happiness we'd enjoyed in our restored relationship. There was none of the guilt or regrets that sometimes hang over people's heads in bereavements and make the grieving process a minefield to move through.

At first there was a *tinge* of sadness: after all, I'd grown to love and appreciate Dad. But the over-riding emotion ever since his death is, purely and simply, one of fond, happy memory.

Reunions of fathers and sons are the stuff of Disney films and parables. Thankfully, it's also the story of real lives like that of Jim, the man I interviewed for our life history project, who came to forgive his father. And the story of my own life. The boy who came home and is still coming home.

For good.

Appendix: Transom Trust

For more information about Transom Trust, the supported accommodation project in Hastings,

Please visit: www.transomtrust.org.uk

Or email: transomtrust@outlook.com

If you would like to make a donation towards the work of Transom Trust, please make payments directly via BACS to:

Account name: Transom Charitable Trust

Sort Code: 09-01-28

Account no: 97752368

28672786R00148

Made in the USA
Columbia, SC
16 October 2018